MW00715030

God Knows
You'd Like
A New Body

God Knows
You'd Like
A New Body

*12 ways to befriend
the one you've got*

Carl Koch and Joyce Heil

SORIN BOOKS   Notre Dame, IN

As publisher of the *GOD KNOWS* series, SORIN BOOKS is dedicated to providing resources to assist readers to enhance their quality of life. We welcome your comments and suggestions, which may be conveyed to:

> SORIN BOOKS
> P.O. Box 1006
> Notre Dame, IN 46556-1006
> Fax: 1-800-282-5681
> e-mail: sorinbk@nd.edu

© 2001 by Carl Koch and Joyce Heil

www.sorinbooks.com

International Standard Book Number: 1-893732-37-1

Cover and text design by Katherine Robinson Coleman.

Printed and bound in the United States of America.

Library of Congress Cataloging-in-Publication Data

Koch, Carl, 1945-
God knows you'd like a new body : 12 ways to befriend the one you've
got / Carl Koch and Joyce Heil.
    p. cm.
    ISBN 1-893732-37-1 (pbk.)
    1. Body, Human--Religious aspects--Christianity. 2.
Self-acceptance--Religious aspects--Christianity. I. Heil, Joyce. II.
Title.
BT741.3 .K63 2001
233'.5--dc21

            2001002436
            CIP

CONTENTS

Introduction

Joyce and I don't watch a lot of television, but the other night we wanted to see a made-for-TV movie that we had heard about. The movie was fine, but what most impressed us were the commercials. In the space of two hours, we were told that we could:

- drop fifty pounds in two months by drinking a diet concoction;

- feel much better if we took designer vitamins;

- smell less and have drier armpits with a particular deodorant;

- sport a full head of hair if we applied a certain chemical application;

- eliminate our hemorrhoids fast and easily, shampoo away our frazzled hair;

- and remove our wrinkles with a secret formula beauty cream.

The irony was not lost on us when other ads tried to lure us into an array of fast food restaurants that, if we ate their offerings, would undoubtedly help us gain weight with their fatty foods!

A million messages bombard us every day about what our body should look like and how we should feel about it. None of the messages offer good news.

If we take what we see and hear seriously, we quickly realize that no body is perfect. Indeed, according to pop culture, no body is even halfway okay except those of a sliver of society composed of high profile models, athletes, and movie stars.

The damage done by the shapers of perception is incalculable: steady increases in the numbers of people suffering from anorexia and bulimia—including more and more boys, millions of dollars spent on fad diets, droves of young men becoming addicted to body-building and "enhancing" supplements, and fear and depression in epidemic proportions. For most of us, the damage is less dramatic, but no less significant: nagging doubts about our looks and decreased self-esteem.

Joyce and I wrote this book because we have been recovering a sense of joy in our bodies, too. It's been a long, difficult journey. We have come to realize that all those cultural messages are rubbish, lies, and deceit.

The body is wonderful, miraculous, amazing, and as God said when creating human beings, "It is good!" In fact, we are made in the image of the Creator. The challenge is to begin accepting ourselves as sacred, beautiful, and good.

Throughout the book, we emphasize "befriending" our body. We like this image for several reasons. First, think of what it means to make a friend. We meet someone, listen to the person's story, share ours, do things together, and spend time with each other. Gradually, as we build our relationship, we grow to care for one another. As a result, we act in the best interests of one another. If our friend is sick, we might come over for a visit and make supper for her or clean her house. If we are celebrating our birthday, she will bring a cake with candles, sing Happy Birthday, and offer a toast. Befriending builds strong bonds that sustain us in tough times and make good times even better.

Another reason we like the term "befriending" is that it implies taking positive action to start a new relationship. Many of us have become so alienated from or dissociated with our bodyself that we need to make the acquaintance with our body all over again. It seems as if many of us either become obsessed with our inadequacy so that our body becomes an enemy, or we become like distant relatives who seldom visit with our body.

Well, this book invites you to befriend your body: no matter how flat- or fleet-footed, bald or bushy haired, Twiggy or Rubenesque you are. Despite the wonders of plastic surgery, most of us will live our whole life with the body we were born in. Why not make a friend of it? The results can be gratifying.

The Process of Befriending

We describe twelve ways of befriending our body. Each of the ways offers reasons or perspective about the way, short quotes for inspiration, and then some reflections or activities that you can use to befriend your body. After the exercises are two stories meant to put flesh and blood on each way.

God Knows You'd Like a New Body is obviously a book to make your way through slowly, thoughtfully, and actively. Keep it by your bed; read a section at night before you drift off to sleep. Spend several days pondering a story or repeating one of the activities. Post one of the short sayings on your bathroom mirror, so that every time you look there you can affirm your bodyself.

In other words, take your time. Making friends takes time and attention. Befriending your body asks no less.

When we make friends with someone, we feel more whole. In fact, the word "health" comes from an Old Saxon word meaning "hale" or "whole." Surely, as we make friends with our body, we will feel integration, not disintegration, ease with ourselves, not dis-ease. Christina Baldwin remarks, "There is something important and healing about deciding to 'come physically home.' The body cannot become part of your spiritual life until you are energetically 'in' it." The stories and sayings, activities and reflections in this book invite you home.

Use the book for healing. Page by page, may you come home to the fullness of yourself.

WAY 1 :

Embrace the Fact That We Do Not Control Everything

LIFE'S UNDER NO OBLIGATION TO
GIVE US WHAT WE EXPECT.

Margaret Mitchell

When my dad put up the basketball hoop over the garage door, I'm not sure what he was thinking. All I knew as a nine-year-old at the time was that the rim seemed miles away. Then, after demonstrating how to shoot, he put the ball in my hands. Of course, wanting to please my dad and be like the big guys in my neighborhood, I would go out and drive for lay-ups, stand at the free throw line painted on the driveway, and shoot and shoot. As I grew older I joined the local Boys' Club teams. Dad would come to the games to encourage me, but I grew convinced that basketball would never be my sport.

In fact, I was growing wide instead of tall. The only way I ever got a rebound was when I used my bulk to bump kids out from under the basket. Then I would spring as high as I could go—maybe five inches off the ground tops—and grab the ball while swinging my elbows. My only notable achievement was accumulating the highest number of fouls of any player at the community center. I didn't mean to foul so much, but my growing heavyweight wrestler's body was never built for basketball.

Nevertheless, I stuck with it well into middle school. Dad and I had some heart to hearts about the game and my limitations. He really did not push me. Mostly he just wanted me to have a winter sport that got me away from adolescent western novels, Tarzan movies on TV, and big bowls of buttered popcorn. Anyway, when the eighth grade basketball season drew to an agonizing close, I hung up my uniform—the one with the adult-size shorts that were a different color (I couldn't fit in any of the regular kids' uniforms) for good. Standing 5'8" and weighing close to 200 pounds, my destiny did not lay in the NBA.

As I have aged, more aspects of my body have instructed me in the stark truth that I just don't have control over a lot about my body. Here are a few of my uncontrollable features:

- I stand 5'10".

- My light complexion means that I better lather my skin with sun block when I'm canoeing for more than fifteen minutes.

- Like the Werners (my mom's family) and Kochs, I have been blessed with a strong, pleasant singing voice.

- I have been taking allopurinol since I was thirty because I inherited a tendency towards gout just like Henry VIII, Samuel Johnson, and Philip II of Spain, all of whom might have been far less cranky if they had this amazing medicine.

- My grandpa and uncles could lift roofing shingles all day. I too have always been able to lift heavy objects.

- I may be the world's cheapest drunk. Despite my bulk, a tiny amount of alcohol puts me rapidly to sleep. This is a trait Joyce and I share, thus we never drink unless we are close to our own bed.

- Like my dear old dad, I started balding right after college.

Sure I could get a toupee. I have tried many diets for my excess weight. But I would still be bald under the rug, and my propensity for being portly has been inherited from lines of stout Germans stretching back for generations. In other words, at some point, I have to admit that I cannot control a lot about my bodyself.

Each of us has a body shaped eons ago by forces beyond our dreaming. For instance, some of us are born Inuits or Eskimos, stocky and compact. Why? Because this body size and short limbs leave less area vulnerable to the harsh cold of the Arctic. Short limbs are ideal for Inuits because blood can warm their extremities much more efficiently. An Eskimo's metabolism is a third higher than a Caucasian's. Their build is perfect for the climate that they have inhabited since time immemorial. Their body has its own wisdom gained in the crucible of centuries.

Clearly our racial and genetic origins play key roles in shaping our particular body. We are a wonderfully unique blending of the genes of our parents, grandparents, and ancestors back to the beginning of humankind. Even with the wonders of modern medicine, we inherit the bodyself that we are.

Then there are our cultural and experiential inheritances. Much of the information given to us about our body is out of our control, too, especially when we are children. Data about our body floods into us from family, friends, enemies, television, and so on. We receive affirmation and insults, falsehoods and truths. And every bit of information can shape our notion of our bodyself. Whole industries thrive trying to help us change ourselves to fit the information that told us we were not quite right. So instead of loving ourselves as we really are, we do a "makeover" or have plastic surgery. Unfortunately, as the terms themselves imply, such attempts at change only address the outside of us. To feel beautiful requires embracing our whole reality.

As with any situation, we have three choices: (1) we can try to change the situation, (2) we can get out of the situation, or (3) we can change our attitude about the situation. Let's face it, most of us are left with choice three.

This third choice, changing our attitude about the situation, can begin when we admit and accept that we don't control everything. Unfortunately, we are trained from an early age to "take charge" or get ourselves "under control." If we carry around extra weight people tell us in so many ways that we lack self-control. If our hair always looks like a bad-hair day, we buy all sorts of sprays and shampoos to get it under control. Women who want to look like Barbie dolls have had dozens of plastic surgeries to sculpt themselves to look like these figurines. Men who want to look like Mr. Universe pump iron for hours each day and gulp questionable supplements.

The trouble is that ultimately, we are not in control. Realizing and accepting this is paradoxically freeing. In other words, when we finally admit that we aren't in control of everything, when we change our attitude to conform to reality, we are making the first choice towards health. We can nurture our body, feed it well, and stay as fit as possible. But finally we are called to love the body *we* have, embrace the reality that *we* are. Like God in the biblical creation story, we may then say, "It is good."

Wood may remain ten years in the water, but it will never become a crocodile.

Congolese proverb

Embrace the Fact That We Do Not Control Everything

- To accept the things we cannot change we might start by reviewing our body inheritance:

  - List parts and features of your body and then name the family member from whom you most likely inherited its characteristics.

  - Write down the names of your parents, grandparents, and great-grandparents. With as much detail as you can remember, describe each one's health history: list the illnesses and conditions each has or had.

  - If you are adopted and do not know your biological parent(s), try to identify any characteristics that make you special and may also predispose you to certain illnesses or conditions.

  - Are there any parts or aspects of your body that you do not particularly like? Spend some time thinking about how you have coped with your feelings.

- Ponder all the aspects of your body that you cannot change. Then, as you think of each one, say the first line of the *Serenity Prayer* used by people in twelve-step recovery programs; use the prayer to recover your power to accept, even love, the body you cannot change: "God, grant me the serenity to accept the things I cannot change."

- Now think about what you can begin to change. List aspects of your physical inheritance that you need to pay attention to: for instance, a family tendency towards diabetes. Then list ways in which your job and home impact your bodily well-being, both in good ways and in unhealthy ways: for instance, a good way—a lot of natural light at home, an unhealthy way—loud noises in the workplace. Next to each unhealthy item, try to describe one way you might change the situation. When you look at your list, you might offer the next line of the *Serenity Prayer*: "God, grant me the courage to change the things I can."

IF WE CANNOT DO WHAT WE WILL,

WE MUST WILL WHAT WE CAN.

Yiddish proverb

The Wisdom to Know the Difference

The Serenity Prayer *asks for help to accept the things we cannot change and courage to change the things that we can. The challenge is the third part of the prayer: the wisdom to know the difference.*

When my mother was diagnosed, the brain tumor had already affected her cognitive abilities. Folks at the elementary school where she taught and was vice principal said that she had seemed confused and, at times, disoriented. And of course, there were the headaches that she had tried to ignore and finally couldn't. But she kept going and was as busy as ever when her last school year ended in May.

My memories of my mother while growing up are of a woman who was continually on the go. She wasn't athletic and didn't exercise, but she always seemed to have some kind of project going, whether something for the local ladies club or the church, or one of her knitting, crocheting, or sewing projects. She also worked on her flower gardens.

However, Mom had been ill on and off during those years. She had contracted tuberculosis and had a lung removed. Three more surgeries for various ailments followed. In those days, we didn't think of holistic medicine and intensive exercise to combat disease. The answer was food. So Mom prepared and ate hearty meals of meat, potatoes, and vegetables with butter. She gained weight and grew into a round, soft mother. Still, she was a beautiful woman and always looked good, never sloppy. Pride in her appearance precluded wearing slacks because of her weight, and she always wore stockings when she left the house.

Mother was proper and insisted on correct manners at meals. She had little tolerance for elbows on the table or picking at food with one's fingers. And even with her weight, she had energy to teach, keep house, and travel with Dad.

As Mom moved into her sixties, she complained more often about being tired, and she mentioned that arthritis was beginning to affect her bones. On the phone she would talk about having good days and bad days. Living so far away and not seeing her often, I was always surprised to hear of fatigue and pain. Since those comments were interlaced with all the things she was doing at school, my image of her remained as the energetic teacher of little children that I had always known.

Then she was diagnosed with a brain tumor. They predicted that she would die within a few months. At the beginning, Mother wouldn't accept the diagnosis. She accepted that she had a brain tumor, but she believed that she would recover. She offered many litanies and prayed many rosaries to bring about a miracle. She was convinced that she was going to recover, drive again, and get back to teaching.

I was living in St. Louis at the time and would fly out to California about every three to four weeks for some treatment she was undergoing or just to visit. The deterioration of her mind and body shocked me. The part of her mind that could calculate and remember immediate events was affected. Her charm and her past memories remained intact. The tumor affected the left side of her body, so her left leg and arm were becoming weaker. The left side of her face sagged as if she had had a stroke.

Mom would cycle through anger and denial of her condition. But I was amazed at how she adjusted to the new normalcy of her deterioration. Initially, she tried to create some craft projects to send to the school. Of course, with only partial use of her left hand, this proved difficult. And one time when I was visiting during her time of radiation therapy, she hurried to the bathroom to throw up. Seeing my worried expression, she just shrugged and said, "This is what I do now."

As time went on, the decline in Mom's body and abilities hastened. Mother, who was so proper at the dining table, ate as if she were voraciously hungry. She would pick up food with her hands and, because of her weakness, food ended up on the table, on her face, and even on the floor. Initially bothered by that lack of control, she gradually seemed more involved in the business of dying.

It wasn't as though she was giving up completely. It was just that the particulars of the body weren't as important to her. She would get angry with God and frustrated at her limitations. However, most of the time she seemed to have accepted that she had no control over her body's deterioration and worked with what she had.

During those months, we all struggled to accept Mom's failing, distorted body, and, of course, her impending death. We couldn't find the sense in this cancer eating away at our mother. She deserved to live into a healthy, happy, and peaceful old age. We railed at not being able to control the disease, not being able to stop it. We cried as the prednisone bloated her body and messed with her brain. But, Mother did die. And she and we could do nothing about it.

Fourteen years later, I don't often think of my mother with her bloated body except when I see pictures of her last few months. I don't even think of my mother as obese, which she was. What I do remember were her hands always in motion when she talked. Hard working hands with ragged nails marked with glue or pen marks from a project she was working on. Then, beautifully manicured hands when she no longer could use them for much.

I remember her smile, gentle and loving or wicked and mischievous. Always with humor. I remember her cajoling and playful charm. She never lost that. And throughout all these years, her indomitable spirit and great gift for loving have remained. She would shake her fist at God and want to control that which couldn't be controlled. But at the end, she seemed to have the wisdom to know the difference, accepting God's love and all that came with her struggle.

Rosalie Hooper-Thomas

ANYTHING IN LIFE THAT WE DON'T ACCEPT WILL SIMPLY MAKE TROUBLE FOR US UNTIL WE MAKE PEACE WITH IT.

Shakti Gawain

Rumania!

We have little control over the makeup of our bodyself, but we can choose how we deal with that fact. I learned this from a former student, now a friend.

"**R**umania! What are you going to do in Rumania of all places," I nearly barked over the phone. My friend Maria was calling from her parent's home in India.

"I'm going to work with orphans. What's so strange about that? You know I've always wanted to do it. I thought you'd be supportive."

I took several deep breaths. I reminded myself that Maria was a grown woman who pulled down a huge salary with a Fortune 500 company in the States and had just completed a multi-million dollar merger agreement between two corporate giants. "Okay, Maria, tell me more."

Maria explained that she had been thinking about this for a long time. In her mid-thirties, unmarried, childless, she had grown weary of the pressures of the high-powered corporate rat race, and she had saved enough to spend two years any way she wanted. As Maria told me more I realized that, in fact, she had the whole adventure well planned out—no surprise, knowing her.

I also knew that Maria loved children, and they felt drawn to her. Besides, Maria was physically unable to have children of her own. That made her decision even more poignant and understandable. So, what could I do but be supportive and encouraging? Still, one worry remained pinned to the back of my throat: What if Maria had an epileptic seizure there and hurt herself? It had happened before, it could happen again. I recalled her story of a seizure hurling her into the line of passengers on a down escalator at a huge shopping mall. Fortunately the mall's security personnel and a couple of shoppers tended to her, but she ended up with a stay in the hospital and a long scar across her forehead. It could have ended much worse.

As if reading my mind, Maria calmly declared. "Look, Carl, I know you're worried about my seizures. Don't be dumb. They have doctors there. I'll take my medications and will be staying with a family that the agency says is really nice. So, cool it. You worry worse than my mother."

Ouch, that hurt. Maria's mother was at once overly cautious about and yet emotionally distant from her daughter. This was the same mother who was so ashamed of her daughter's epilepsy that she had hid Maria's condition from even aunts and uncles. Indeed, Maria's parents had sent her off to posh boarding schools and to a university in the United States and Canada at least in part so that no one would know about her epilepsy. Over the many years that I had known her, Maria had shared this sad story in bits and pieces.

But Maria was a survivor. She carried on a full schedule with the constant possibility of debilitating seizures that could knock her down anywhere, any-time, and had. And, by the time she was thirty, she had also endured breast cancer and two partial mastec-tomies. Maria lived with the knowledge that breast cancer had killed three close family members in their thirties and could come back at any time.

Maria had no control over the epilepsy. No control over the cancer. She lived with both. So everywhere she had moved, she drew a circle of wonderful friends close around her. Her brilliant mind for finances and sheer hard work landed her interesting and lucrative jobs. Multinational companies tried to recruit her. And she traveled widely. Business took her to Switzerland, Japan, Australia, and all over North America. Adventure lured her to Greece, China, England, and Peru.

Despite the lingering anguish about her relationship with her family back home in India, Maria managed. Managed well. Still, she wanted more than a luxury condominium and a big salary. The thousands of abandoned, sick children of Rumania beckoned.

The night before she left we talked by phone. My interrogation calmed some of my nerves. She sounded much less anxious than I was, but then I realized that she would survive moving to a poor country, living simply, and giving aid to sick children. "Look, Carl," she said soothingly, "I'll do fine. Remember, I've seen poverty. Besides, I can't wait. I've been given so many gifts. I've had it so good, I just want to give some of that back."

I waited to hear from her. And waited. After a couple of months, I wondered if something had happened. I told myself that if I had not heard anything by the end of that week, I would check in with the sponsoring agency.

Friday of that week, I opened my mailbox, ready to be disappointed again. But, I spotted a thick, ragged, blue envelope from Maria under the stack of junk mail. Tossing down the other mail, I quickly slit the envelope open. A dozen photos spilled out. Gathering them up, I slowly studied each one. Maria's smiling face mashed up against the dirty cheek of a thin child laughing with her. Laughing Maria holding a giggling child with Down's syndrome. And on and on. Then I opened her letter:

> Dear Carl,
>
> Sorry that I've been so slow in writing. As you can see, I've been busy with my kids. Don't you love them!
>
> I can read your mind. No seizures, and a good doctor is in town here. Stop worrying. I don't have any control of all that anyway. Life goes on.

Since pictures speak a thousand words, I'll keep this short. I love it here. I love the kids, my host family, and the 12-hour days. Who knows, when I come home I may have a couple of these little urchins in tow (wanted to give you something to worry over).

I'm happy.

Love,

Maria

Life goes on indeed, I thought. And I was happy, too.

THERE IS NO GOOD IN ARGUING WITH THE INEVITABLE. THE ONLY ARGUMENT AVAILABLE WITH AN EAST WIND IS TO PUT ON YOUR OVERCOAT.

James Russell Lowell

Tell Your Body's Story: The Whole Truth & Nothing But the Truth

---

TURNING THE ATTENTION TO THE BODY IS THE BEGINNING OF THE PROCESS OF COMPASSIONATE SELF-CARE.

Stephen R. Schwartz

K nowing that she certainly was not considered attractive bothered the little girl, but as she entered late adolescence her attitude about herself underwent a transformation. Later in her life she declared that she realized that not being seen as beautiful was actually a blessing in disguise: "It forced me to develop inner resources and strength. I came to understand that women who can't lean on their beauty must work harder to have the advantage." The girl grew up to be Golda Meir, the prime minister of Israel.

We know James Earl Jones as the great actor he is. Besides his many starring roles in films and on stage, Jones was the voice of Darth Vader in the *Star Wars* movies and King Mufasa in *The Lion King*. What only a small circle of people realize is that James Earl Jones has stuttered since childhood and still finds spontaneous public speaking quite difficult.

"You keep the stuttering under control because you have a script," Jones remarked. "In real life, I just try to get through the day or through the conversation. I'm not good in talk-show interviews. I will think of something that might be brilliant to say, and I can't get it worded."

Pearl Bailey once said, "There's a period of life when we swallow a knowledge of ourselves, and it becomes either good or sour inside." However, first we need to face the facts about ourselves. We need to sit down and tell ourselves the truth about our body's story.

The story of our body goes back even before we arrived on the planet as a wet and wizened newborn. Our parents inherited features from their parents, and their parents the same before them. Thus, we arrive predisposed to be athletes or actors, redheads or brunettes, mathematicians or musicians. Our genetic makeup means that we may be prone to trimness or obesity, diabetes or certain cancers, high blood pressure or anemia.

Still, we certainly have a lot to say about the rest of our body's story. Perhaps we once enjoyed hiking in the mountains and now find walking to the street corner a bit much. Maybe surgeries have left scars crisscrossing our torso. Or maybe we woke up at age forty and decided that we were tired of carrying around all that extra weight, so we learned to eat well, started aerobics, and began competitive square dancing.

When we first visit a new doctor, she or he will always want a medical history. They ask about medications, accidents, illnesses, exercise, surgeries, and incidences of certain conditions in our family. A good place to begin loving our body is to complete such a history for us. After all, real love must be rooted in knowledge.

Telling our body's story can even be an adventure. Journalist Demetria Martinez tells about recording her story truthfully:

> My body used to be what happened between deep thoughts and peak emotions. Until I became ill. Or, more correctly, until I began to seek a diagnosis for symptoms that had plagued me for a decade.
>
> Fate demanded I no longer treat my body like an apartment rented for life, with the hope that, should anything break, a landlord will come fix it.
>
> And so I set out to familiarize myself with, well, myself.

Like many of us, Demetria Martinez's initial impulse toward healing began out of pain, but it turned into an adventure of discovery. First, she started exploring the story of her body. Then she began making decisions to treat her body differently. The end result? Healing.

Both my parents are dead now. And I can pretty well predict how I will pass on too. Most likely I will eventually have something go wrong with my ticker. Both Mom and Dad died of heart failure at age eighty-five. Most of my aunts and uncles died similarly, well into their eighties. Last year I started taking medication for mild hypertension, which reflects my own story of being stressed by work and a lifetime of obesity. That has been a major part of my body story. But it need not be my fate.

I realized that unless I did something about my weight, even though my cholesterol was okay and stress test results normal, I would likely be looking at increased chances of heart trouble, circulation problems, high blood pressure, and so on. On the other hand, my story has also included canoeing winding rivers, hiking in the Sangre de Cristo Mountains, and swimming at the fitness center where Joyce and I go nearly every day.

Joyce was on anti-hypertensives for more than twenty years, and her cholesterol was creeping up along with her weight. Her story includes grandparents who died early of heart failure, and her dad's heart is none too good.

So last July Joyce and I both decided to learn how to eat better and to begin exercising more regularly. When we put our canoe in the water recently, it road a hundred pounds higher in the water. Our bills from the pharmacist are half of what they were and, God willing, we will be free from them altogether in a few more months. Best of all we feel better and have more energy for the things we like to do. Our dog, Daisy, complains about our longer, brisker walks, but they are good for her, too.

We are all likely familiar with the adage: "Those who ignore history are condemned to repeat it." This old saying was true when we first heard it from our high school history teacher. It is just as true about our body's story. Joyce and I try not to fret over our past. However, when we started coming to grips with the downsides of our story, we began moving towards health of body and peace of mind. The upsides of our body story—canoeing, walking our pooch, working in the garden—are now even more enjoyable.

Friendships start with knowledge. We find out where the other person is from, who their family is, what they do for a job, and so on; in short, what their story is. To befriend our body, we can start by honestly reviewing our body's story. Just as becoming friends is an adventure, so is befriending our body.

Now is the acceptable time for us to start sorting through our body story. Our story is not our fate, and the adventure of telling our story can lead to acceptance, healing, and love.

SELF-KNOWLEDGE IS THE BEGIN-
NING OF SELF-IMPROVEMENT.

Spanish proverb

Tell Your Body's Story

- Compose a list of the most important events in your body's story. So that you do not forget any essential happening, you might write your list by periods of five or ten years: for instance, one to ten, eleven to twenty years of age, and so on. Briefly describe the important "body event" and then the physical and emotional effects that you experienced as a result: for instance, "Orthoscopic knee surgery made me more cautious when playing tennis, almost ruined my game, and made me decide to either play hard or quit, I gradually stopped altogether and started swimming."

- Find pictures of your mother, father, siblings, grandparents, aunts, and uncles. If possible, seek pictures from your childhood, adolescence, young adulthood, and various stages of your adulthood. Looking at each family member, ask yourself: Did she or he like her or his body? How did they demonstrate their feelings about their bodyself? What did I learn from my family about my own body? What did they say and how did they act about my body? Am I holding on to what my family taught me about my body? How did I feel about my body at each stage of life? Looking at pictures of myself, how did I feel about my body at the time of each picture?

- List the names of people who affirmed or accepted your bodyself, and then list names of people who had a negative impact on your body image. Try to specify how each person helped or hurt.
- Ponder one central event from your life that, for you, summarizes the story of your body.

IF YOU WANT TO CHANGE WHAT
OTHER PEOPLE THINK OF YOU, YOU
MUST CHANGE WHAT YOU THINK OF
YOURSELF.

George Bernard Shaw

Not Everyone Can Be Big-Busted— Shall We Get On With Our Lives?

As Leslie Knowlton tells the story of accepting her breasts, she describes how this growing awareness helped her accept her whole body.

It was probably about the age of twelve that I became aware of my own less-than-voluptuous chest and got a bit concerned.

The original impetus for worry was, of course, males. As the only girl in a family of five children, I'd long prided myself on being one of the boys. And the boys I knew liked me fine because my assets then were bravery, batting ability, and being able to outrun any of them. Yet I couldn't help noticing when other girls began getting attention for breasts that I didn't have.

Actually, the main male magnet was Diana, a new kid in school whose curves, at thirteen, rivaled those of any centerfold. From the minute she showed up that first morning in eighth grade, I watched once derring-do boys switch to vacant staring and, worse, inane giggling. I adjusted to the new milieu by becoming Diana's best friend. And while I had my share of teenage heartache, I never blamed any of the pain on the size of my chest.

Yet I did all the silly breast stuff girls are wont to do, such as ordering a pink plastic bust contraption and exercising for hours every week, with no detectable results.

But thanks to the go-natural craze of the late sixties and early seventies, I stopped concerning myself with finding bras I could fill. I threw away the ones I had and, for the first time, felt totally uninhibited and free— an attitude that attracted men like crazy. Nor did I dress to hide my now-unencumbered breasts as I floated around in diaphanous blouses and flower-child skirts.

When the eighties hit and silicone implants became the rage, I paid no heed, even though I'd moved to body-beautiful Southern California. Instead, I enrolled in both a gym and grad school, exercising what nature did grant me a strong torso, shapely legs, a reasonable mind. I still fancied myself a free spirit and rarely felt self-conscious about my bust. I wasn't modest when undressing in the locker room (not that I wanted to show off my breasts; I simply didn't focus on them as sexual objects).

And yet . . . and yet . . . despite this generally happy state, I wasn't completely immune to attacks of insecurity. Being small chested meant I had to stay thin lest I whack out of proportion, so perhaps I did envy some women with ample bosoms. My friend Nancy, a Rubenesque blonde, looked so pretty and feminine, so languidly lush. I admit I sometimes felt less than womanly when I was around her.

Next came marriage and pregnancy and, as my mother's had, my mammaries worked just fine. I nursed for a year and a half with B-cup breasts and afterward was shocked to see them shrink. Thankfully, being a journalist who wrote stories about more pressing concerns—such as life-threatening disease—helped keep my I'm-okay perspective intact.

But then the nineties arrived and everything changed. Suddenly, I found myself subtly aware of my breast size in a way I'd never been before. The self-doubt lurked like some insidious undiagnosed tumor. Perhaps I felt so strange because I was newly divorced and found myself alone in a nightmare single's world. Everyone seemed too young and too perfect. Or maybe I'd just been fooling myself all those years.

Feeling ill, I left the apartment in search of Brazilian-looking men, and that's when I saw—sitting smack-center in a shop window—*Intrigue*, silicone pouches to be worn in one's bra. I went into the store to feel the polyurethane-covered blobs, priced at eighty dollars the pair. "They're our hottest item," a saleswoman trilled when she saw me handling the merchandise. "These are much cheaper and safer than surgery. They pass the hug test too." I returned home and felt my breasts. They were getting smaller. They didn't seem perky and young anymore. They looked . . . missing.

I decided to give *Intrigue* a try. So the next night found me heading to the theater decked out in a black knit dress and black *Intrigue*-loaded bra. I felt like a bombshell, and as I walked through the theater lobby, men did stare at my chest. I was experiencing what I never had before: attention because of my breast size, which made me feel like a different person. And I hated that!

I've worked too hard to try to be comfortable with who I am to give up now. I have to know that men (and women) are seeing the real me, the one who's trying to love herself the way she is, because I believe the greatest success comes with self-acceptance.

Besides, I've managed these many years with my own breasts. And overall, I've gotten along quite well—not in spite of or even because of my chest but thanks to the whole gestalt of me. While breasts may attract, they certainly don't guarantee love, happiness, or healthy self-esteem. Plus, as Eleanor Roosevelt said, "No one can make you feel inferior without your consent."

So that night I ended my Mr. Toad's Wild Detour Into Self-Doubt. I laughingly bade my bomber breasts a fond farewell, thanking them for lessons learned. But I didn't throw them away. I'm using them as paperweights. They're holding down my tickets to Brazil.

Leslie Knowlton

FREEDOM IS WHAT YOU DO WITH
WHAT'S BEEN DONE TO YOU.

Jean-Paul Sartre

Birthing a New Self-Image

Giving birth to our new self-image has its roots in telling and accepting our unique story. It often takes time and conscious effort.

Perhaps when I was very young I loved and trusted my body. But somewhere along the way, I began to believe that my body was weak, clumsy, and untrustworthy. When I started school, I learned that my body would not run fast, did not know how to throw or catch balls. I was the last one picked for every team. Eventually, I came to accept that my body was somehow defective. Though seldom sick, it just could not perform well.

I learned to avoid any situation that would highlight my physical ineptitude. So I grew physically cautious: I only learned to ride a bike when I was eighteen and headed off to college. To make matters worse, as I grew older, my body embarrassed me further as I got taller and more voluptuous than my friends did.

This body image matched my mother's. She judged her body as too tall, too heavy, and unattractive. Mother avoided sports except for occasional walks and swims. She concentrated on perfecting her mind, and so did I.

During the required phys-ed classes in college, I learned with amazement that I could master athletic skills when someone bothered to teach me. Even so, my foray into sports was short-lived. I reverted back to self-doubt, caution. Like my mother, I walked and swam. In my late twenties during a rush of romantic enthusiasm, my husband and I took ballroom dancing classes. Eventually anxiety about my agility and worries about goofing up the steps blocked my enjoyment.

Then at age thirty-two, after agonizing deliberations, I decided to have a child. I fretted that my body wasn't up to the task, so I joined a health club, changed my diet, and got into training for pregnancy and childbirth. I wanted to be a worthy bearer of this new life.

I was astonished by my strong emotional reaction when I found out that I was pregnant. Suddenly I was a walking miracle, Earth Mother herself, acutely aware of the life growing inside me, feeling connected to generations of women before me. I was euphoric. Even so, I approached with trepidation each appointment with my midwife. Was I doing it right?

Gradually, as my pregnancy progressed, my anxiety drained away. I listened, fascinated, in awe of my baby's heartbeat. When the baby kicked and my stomach jumped out, wonder overwhelmed me. Later in the pregnancy, I could spot the outline of a little heel, popping against the stretched skin.

My baby grew, and my belly stretched bigger and bigger, adapting to the growing infant inside. That I had little control over this growing dawned on me. Then when labor began and continued for days without any acknowledgement of my desire for hastening it, I knew in my bones that life was in charge, not me.

Finally, as hard labor set in at the hospital, I let go and allowed myself to be swept into the current that had overtaken me. While part of me was breathing, laboring just as birthing required, another part of me watched amazed by this ancient force, powerful and imperative. I was not birthing my baby. The ancient wisdom of my female body was. Strong. I felt strong, filled with the power of the universe.

Holding my newborn, glorious child after the long birth, I realized that the whole journey of my pregnancy changed forever the way I felt about my body. For the first time in my life, I felt strong. For the first time in my life, I had let go, trusting the ancient wisdom in my body. I—my bodyself—proved competent, capable, powerful.

And so, I wondered what else my bodyself could do. For almost thirteen years now I've been learning. And the lessons are all good.

Anne Peek

WE ARE GOD'S WORK OF ART.

Paul of Tarsus

WAY 3:

Be Present
Where You Are

THE QUALITY OF LIFE IS IN
PROPORTION, ALWAYS, TO THE
CAPACITY FOR DELIGHT. THE
CAPACITY FOR DELIGHT IS THE GIFT
OF PAYING ATTENTION.

Julia Cameron

F ear and stress about our body, our job, our relationships—about anything—usually have their origins
in worrying over the future: What's going to happen?
What will people think? Will I look okay? Am I too fat?
Am I too tall? So then we learn over and over that none
of this worry gets us anywhere but sick.

While reviewing our story provides insights into
our present attitudes, fears, worries, and tendencies,
we examine it so that we can consciously let go of it, so
that we are not victimized by automatic, learned behav-
ior that may not be healthy for us. We will learn to love,
appreciate, and effectively care for our bodyself when
we let go of the past and pay attention to the present.
We will improve the quality of our life and the joy of

our body when we simply pay close attention to the now, withholding judgments, and just being present.

Russian writer Leo Tolstoy told a story about being present where we are. It goes like this:

A young king needed to find out the answers to three questions: How do I do the right thing at the right time? Whose advice do I believe? How do I set priorities so that I do the most important thing first? When he had posed these questions to his court advisers, they left him frustrated because they just told him what they thought he wanted to hear.

The king had heard about a wise hermit who lived deep in the forest. So one day he dressed in the clothes of a commoner and went to find the hermit and, hopefully, find the answers to his three questions.

The young king finally found the hermit who was digging in his garden. The king posed the three questions to the wise old man, but he did not answer. Indeed, the hermit could barely stand up. Seeing the distress of the hermit, the king took the old man's shovel and finished digging his garden. Just as he completed the work, a stranger entered the clearing and collapsed. Blood flowed from a stomach wound inflicted on the intruder by one of the king's guards posted in the woods.

The king immediately cleaned the wound, bandaged it with pieces of his own clothing, and continued to change the bandages until the bleeding ceased. Then he moved the wounded stranger into the hermit's hut. Since night had fallen, the king slept on the floor nearby so that he could attend to the stranger and the hermit.

Upon waking in the morning, the king overheard the wounded man confess to the hermit that he had been hiding in the woods, hoping to assassinate the king who had once handed down a judgment against his family. Even after hearing this, the king assured the would-be assassin that he would have his personal physician look after him.

The king prepared to leave the hermit, but posed his three questions again. To the king's surprise, the hermit told the king that he had already received answers to all three questions during the previous day. The hermit explained: When the king saw that the hermit could not finish turning his garden, the king completed the work for him. That was the right thing to do at the right moment. Had the king left just then, his enemy would have killed him in the woods. When the wounded stranger staggered into the clearing, the king cleaned and bandaged the wound, thus doing the right thing at the right time. In doing so he had transformed an enemy into a friend.

"So," concluded the hermit, "only one time is important: *right now!* Moreover, the most important people are those whom you are with. That which is of highest priority is to do good to the people in front of you. Doing good is the sole reason that we are sent into this life." And the king returned to his court satisfied.

In many respects those of us who have a hard time accepting, let alone loving, our bodies have the same questions that the young king had. They might be stated this way:

How do I know what the right approach is to my body and when I can start loving it?

For instance, if we are overweight we might fret that if we learn to love our body, we will not be motivated to lose the extra pounds. If we finally accept our attractive features, we worry that we might come off as proud. I suspect the hermit would reply, "There's no time like the present. Love yourself, body and all. Do well for your body by paying attention to what it's telling you, eating well, and exercising adequately. Now is the right time."

Whose advice should I listen to?

Well, I'm sure that the hermit would have little use for what most of the popular media would advise about the body. He would likely urge us to pay attention to what our own brains and feelings tell us and stop worrying about what others might say.

Where should I start—what's my priority—in learning to love my bodyself?

The wise old hermit would repeat what he told the king: "The most important place to start with is what's in front of you now." So, if we are eating, we eat, slowly enjoying each bite. If we are walking, we walk, conscious of the wonder of walking. If we are making love, we are only making love, not worrying about missing our tee time or getting the children to school. If we are buying clothes, we attend to how we feel about the clothes, not wondering what so-and-so will think.

We love our body by first being in our body: paying attention, being present where we are. Not only will our stress levels decline and our blood pressure descend, but also our levels of appreciation and care will increase. As Eleanor Roosevelt said, the choice is ours: "In the long run we shape our lives and we shape ourselves. The process never ends until we die. And the choices we make are ultimately our responsibility." A key choice—for the young king, for Eleanor Roosevelt, for us, for you—is to care for ourselves, body and spirit, right now, as we are. This is the right thing to do and the right time.

YOUR LIFE IS THE SUM OF YOUR
PRESENT MOMENTS, SO IF YOU'RE
MISSING LOTS OF THEM, YOU MAY
ACTUALLY MISS MUCH OF YOUR
LIFE.

Jon Kabat-Zinn

Be Present Where You Are

- This exercise invites you to simply pay attention to your body. Just be aware or mindful of your body. It can be done anywhere: a waiting room, on a commuter train, or lying in bed right before sleep. The purpose is to spend a few moments being in touch with your body, just as it is. Close your eyes. Relax. Breathe deeply and slowly, focusing on every breath coming in and going out. Then beginning with your head and moving down, become conscious of every part of your body. Do not *think* about your body; rather, try to simply *feel* it, all parts of it, every sensation you can. Feel the touch of your hair against your forehead or ears or neck. Become aware of the touch of your clothes on your shoulder. Focus for a moment on the touch of your back against the chair . . . the shirt or blouse on your arms . . . your hands touching one another or resting on your lap . . . your buttocks and thighs touching the chair or floor . . . your feet within your shoes or against the floor.

Repeat the exercise: head . . . shoulders . . . arms . . . right hand . . . left hand . . . thighs . . . feet. Repeat it again. Continue to go around, moving from one part of your body to another. Be mindful of each part for just a few seconds. Keep moving from one to the other. When you are ready to end, thank your Creator for the gift of your body. Be mindful all day of its wonderful workings.

* This exercise honors the *now* and affirms our presence in this moment without the worries of the past or concerns for the future. It can last for as long as you wish, anywhere, anytime, in any position. Focusing on our breathing calms us, slows our heart rate, and yet is energizing. By choosing to consciously smile, we affirm the goodness of the present moment. Smiling relaxes us, partly because we use twice as many muscles to frown. Since the purpose of the exercise is to pay attention and affirm the present moment, you might keep your eyes open. Breathe slowly, deeply, and evenly.

  * During one or two breaths say:

    "Breathing in, I calm my body."

    "Breathing out, I smile."

  * After one or two breaths, continue for about fifteen breaths:

    Breathing in say, "Calm."

    Breathing out say, "Smile."

Continue until you feel calm, relaxed, and ready for phase two:

  * During one or two breaths say:

    "Breathing in, I live in the present moment."

    "Breathing out, I know it is a wonderful moment."

  * After one or two breaths, continue for as long as you like:

Breathing in say, "Present moment."
Breathing out say, "Wonderful moment."

(This exercise is adapted from *The Blooming of the Lotus* by Thich Nhat Hanh.)

- You can practice being present where you are while you do any task. For instance, when you are doing housework, just do one thing at a time. As you scrub the toilet, just scrub the toilet. As you vacuum the living room carpet, concentrate on vacuuming. If you become distracted just remind yourself gently, "I am vacuuming now." Thus, housework becomes a kind of meditation. Besides, you work more efficiently when you do one thing at a time. When you finish cleaning, take a moment or two to appreciate all of the complex abilities of your body to do these tasks.

- Another practice of mindfulness of your body can happen when bathing or showering. Allow yourself a longer time to take a bath or shower. Prepare for the bath or shower carefully. As you clean, do so consciously, slowly, appreciatively. Notice your skin, the feel of the water, soap, and wash cloth. Pay attention to every part of your body. If you start to judge or fret over some part, let the worry or judgment go. Just be present. When you finish, you might be surprised at how clean your mind and emotions are, too. Take a few moments to give thanks for your body, just as it is.

SANITY PROCLAIMS THAT IMMEDIATE AWARENESS IS SIMPLY A STATE OF APPRECIATION. . . . IMMEDIATE AWARENESS IS THE CLEAR CLEAN AIR WITHOUT WHICH HEALING AND GROWTH ARE STUNTED.

Gerald May

A Rose by Any Other Name

One Friday afternoon right after lunch, as the nursing department meeting dragged on, I found myself beginning to doze. Then I heard giggles. Then laughter. At first I thought that I had been spotted drifting off into the land of nod, but when I looked down the long table I realized the source of the merriment. Rose had donned a giant, blinking red nose. As if nothing was out of the ordinary, she sat calmly making remarks—which no one really heard—about the issue at hand. People complimented her on her new nose, but some said that they liked her blinking reindeer antlers better. Once again, Rose had succeeded in waking all of us up.

Rose always seems to be awake, attentive, and alive. Sixty-something, Rose is the senior member of our department—chronologically at least. She certainly acts much younger. Rose has a lively sense of humor, but she is also a consummate professional. She constantly studies, keeping up with the latest research in nursing. Rose chairs the local area nurses' association and does wonders advising students that the rest of us find hard to reach. Even with her busy schedule of teaching, advising, committee, and volunteer work, Rose fits in a jazzercise class three times a week and always manages to walk her dog. She is certainly one of my role models.

What makes Rose so amazing is that she does all she does while living with a critical medical condition: Crohn's disease, a chronic inflammation of the bowels that is periodically debilitating and can, in some instances, prove fatal.

I asked her once how she stayed so alive. Her answer was as simple as it is profound: "I live in awe of the present moment." Then she told me this:

My life changed when I was fifteen. Before that I had been a well child. During my sophomore year, I became mysteriously ill with what we now know is Crohn's disease. We tried all the usual home remedies and, since it was Christmas break, I took it easy. Nothing helped. After many visits to the doctor, he decided that an appendectomy might work. It didn't. By summer I was in bad shape. So they put me in the hospital.

After nine weeks in the hospital, they sent me home to recover. Right before Christmas I got to spend half a day at school. Eventually I started full-time again.

All those weeks of pain taught me several things. First, I learned about the goodness of people. Relatives, neighbors, teachers, my parents' friends, and members of our church visited, brought gifts, and sent cards. Several people sent "theme cards" each day for a week. Their kindness amazed me.

The second lesson was how healing it was to be out in nature. After weeks indoors, I found it wonderful just being outside. My parents would often take me for long drives so I could view the fall colors and smell the damp woodsy fragrance. Ever since then, I try to enjoy every season—the small wonders like daisies blooming, sun shining on a lake, and of course my pooch. Even during my long illness, I would surprise people with my enthusiasm about sunrises or ladybugs. I was sad sometimes that they looked at these same things with eyes that seemed to say "ho-hum."

Anyway, the other lesson I learned was that life is precious and fragile, so I better enjoy it right now. So I do. For about twenty years, I stayed healthy enough. Then in my thirties I had several more surgeries for various complications and then long convalescences. Again, my belief in the kindness of people and the goodness of each moment only got stronger.

Funny how I ended up being a nurse. When I had my appendix out, I wanted to be a nurse because the student nurses seemed to have so much fun. My long confinement in the hospital killed my enthusiasm for nursing. But then I read a book by a nurse who studied people who had survived serious illnesses like mine and concluded that once they had recovered, most of them had come to the same realization that I had: Life is filled with wonderful moments.

I wouldn't wish Crohn's disease on anyone, myself included. Still, many years ago, I stopped longing for a different life than the one I have now. While higher level wellness would have been more comfortable, maybe the experience of really appreciating the wonders of life in the present moment would not have been given to me in exchange.

With that, Rose smiled, cracked the latest joke she got from an e-mail, and headed off to her next class. I was left wondering what sort of nose or funny mask she would bring to our next meeting, and at Rose herself.

Joyce Heil

IF WE LIVE GOOD LIVES, THE TIMES ARE ALSO GOOD. AS WE ARE, SUCH ARE THE TIMES.

Augustine of Hippo

Consider the Lilies

When I travel, I like to bring treasures home with me. I have four carved wooden masks from Kenya and a small Buddha I found in Katmandu. I have an eyeglass case made out of frog skin from China, a prayer rug from Turkey, and two woven reed baskets from Ethiopia. I collected so much booty in Israel that I had to ship it home in three separate boxes. I prize my icons from Jericho, my first-century glass goblets, and my Bedouin silver bracelet. When I handle these things they stir my memory of places I've been.

It is true that much of what I remember are the shops where I purchased them. In Katmandu, the mask came from the same shop where black market money exchanges were made. Hundred dollar bills brought the best rate, and there was such a long line of tourists outside the shop that it is a wonder we were not all busted. The rug purchase required hours of formal negotiation, fueled by obligatory glasses of sweet Turkish coffee.

In China, transactions took place in the street. As soon as the local people saw my companions and me they surrounded us and held out all sorts of wondrous things for our consideration. There was an antique opium pipe with a brass bowl and a jade stem. There were ivory chopsticks in an embroidered silk case. There were traditional baby bonnets with antennae and colorful pompoms on them to scare away malicious spirits.

Since none of us spoke the language, it was unclear how much these things cost. Finally one of us offered the equivalent of three dollars for a pair of embroidered slippers, and the crowd exploded. Some people ran to get more things to sell us while others pushed their goods in our faces. They were all talking at once, each trying to drown the other out. When I spied an opening in the throng, I escaped. A quiet woman carrying a baby followed me and sold me the frog skin case.

This past summer, my destination was the mountains of northern Greece, in a remote region called Zagoria that is just making it onto the tourist maps. The Vikos Gorge is there, along with Smolikas, the second-highest mountain in Greece. The itinerary promised a week of hard hiking, with evenings spent in different villages each night.

The first day the scenery absorbed me. It was the day of a solar eclipse, which made the air look speckled when our small group stopped for lunch by a slow-flowing river. The water was so blue it looked dyed. The beach was made of round stones, which felt fine under bare feet that had suffered for hours in heavy boots. After a meal of fresh tomatoes, cucumbers, salami, and feta cheese, we filled our water bottles from a spring that poured through the roots of an old plane tree. Then we talked until we fell asleep, napping in the smooth stones that cradled our lazy bodies like a magic finger mattresses.

By the second day I was ready to shop. The village where we would spend the night was supposed to be popular with Greek tourists. I envisioned streets lined with shops that sold silver, icons, and carved wooden objects. Instead, I discovered a quiet town with about a dozen pensions and one very good restaurant. There was absolutely nothing to buy except a few postcards and ice cream on a stick.

The same thing happened in the next village and the next. Slowly I realized that I was in a time warp, among people who did not equate having a good time with buying things. I could walk in the mountains by day and listen to bouzouki music in the town square by night. I could talk for hours over meals of souvlaki and retsina, and I could let the villagers teach me to dance, but I could not shop. There was no T-shirt, no necklace, no salad bowl necessary to make this experience complete. It required no accessories. It was mine for the living of it, and when I got home I would have nothing to show for it but the stories.

Charmed as I was by this wisdom, I was unable to accept it entirely. Before I knew it, I was shopping for stones as I walked each day, searching the path for any with especially fine color or shape. When I found one, I would hold it until I found a better one. This meant that I almost missed the pair of Egyptian vultures that sailed briefly overhead, and I did not see the shallow alpine lake until I almost stepped in it, but the truth is that I did not want to consider the lilies. I wanted something more permanent that would help me avoid the knowledge that my life, like the lilies, is so sweet but fragile—here today and gone tomorrow—with no purchasable protection from that fact.

As we climbed higher, the stones began to look alike. Trees gave way to bushes, bushes to grasses. Finally there was nothing but loose shale underfoot as we trudged toward the mountain hut where we would spend the night. That was when I looked down and saw one tiny red flower blooming in the brown dust at my feet. Since Greece gets no rain in August, it must have survived on dew. A little further I saw a yellow flower—just one—and after that a white one, nestled in the shadow of a stone. They were all so different, and so improbably alive. Compared to them, rocks were cheap. Rocks would always be there, while these small beauties held nothing back. It was now or never for them. I could love them or not—the choice was mine—but I could not own them. They were not made for that.

Barbara Brown Taylor

WAKE AT DAWN WITH A WINGED HEART AND GIVE THANKS FOR ANOTHER DAY OF LOVING.

Kahlil Gibran

WAY 4:

Accept What You Feel, Then Decide to Feel Good

WE CANNOT CHANGE ANYTHING UNLESS WE ACCEPT IT.

Carl Jung

Rosie O'Donnell defies the stereotype of most movie or television personalities. She tends towards being stout, wears what she wants, and most of all speaks her mind without worrying what her publicist will say. In an interview with *Radiance*, a magazine for big women, Rosie remarked,

> When I read in the newspaper that some radio jock says, "She's so fat and gross" it hurts my feelings. I sometimes get out of the shower and think, Oh, boy, I have to do something. And then I have to work hard to stand in front of the mirror after that image goes through, and say, "This is who you are, and this is where you are. You're okay in this body, and you're a great, healthy, lovable, and loving person, and go forward with love." And that's

49

what I try to do . . . I just try to accept myself for where I am. I don't always succeed, but I try, especially in what I present to the media, because I know little kids are watching.

Rosie provides a great example to kids and to the rest of us of someone who has appraised her body and accepted her feelings about it.

Another person who has accepted his body was an anonymous one-legged man that writer Anne Peek met quite by accident one day. She shares:

> After enjoying a pleasant lunch with my husband, he had gone to get the car to pick me up. I hummed to myself and gently bobbed to my inner music as I stood out of the rain under the restaurant's awning. Just then I noticed a man approaching on crutches. He looked ordinary enough, except that he only had one leg. He maneuvered his crutches expertly. When he reached the restaurant door, I said "hello" and opened the door for him.
>
> "You're in a good mood," he answered with a smile. Then looking at my feet, he asked, "How do you like your shoes?"
>
> A bit startled, I glanced down at my sturdy walking shoes. "Fine."
>
> "Where did you get them?"
>
> I told him.
>
> "I got some like that at Nordstrom's. After the salesman found some to fit me I asked him if I could buy just one. After all, I can only use one," he grinned, pointing to his missing leg.
>
> "The sales guy talked to his boss, and they agreed. So then I told him that since I was only buying one shoe, it should be half price." He waited for a moment for that to sink in.
>
> "They said yes, so I went back the next week and bought two more pair—just one

shoe, you know. And they were half-priced,"
he said with a smile.

Before I could say anything, he chuckled
and added, "I told Dayton's what
Nordstrom's did, and so they had to do it,
too."

"Have a great day!" With that he disap-
peared into the restaurant. I don't think he
heard my, "Thank you. You, too."

My husband drove up. Marveling at the
man's spirit, I slipped into the front seat.

Our bodies come in all shapes, sizes, and colors,
even though our genetic makeup is mostly the same.
Our body images—the way in which we perceive our
body—results from mega-bites of data that we learn
from events and relationships over the courses of our
lives. Some of us have received more positive information about ourselves than negative; for others the situation is reversed. The sum of all those perceptions forms
our image of our body.

Clearly, Rosie O'Donnell and the man with one leg
have decided to accept their bodies. Each has looked at
her or his own body and declared, "It is good." Not
perfect. Not the stereotypical ideal. But, good.

Sometimes, like Rosie, we might have to stop,
reflect, and feel what we feel about our body, especially when the messages we get are negative. No one can
"make us feel" anything. We feel what we feel. If we
don't like the way we feel, we can decide to feel differently. The key is to accept and affirm who we are,
declaring even through the doubts and fears, "I am
good. My body is good."

The self we need to love is our own self, not someone else's. An old story relates how the revered Rabbi
Zusya had finally arrived at the end of his long life. His
followers gathered around his bedside to console him,
to pray the psalms, and to perhaps hear his final words
of wisdom. They knew that the moment of his death

would soon arrive, so one of them softly asked him for a parting message. A hush fell over the room. In a failing voice, Rabbi Zusya uttered his last words, "In the next world, they will not ask me, 'Why were you not Moses?' They will ask me, 'Why were you not Zusya?'"

Why were you not Carl? Why were you not Joyce? We were not created to be other than ourselves, with our good body, our good set of talents and gifts, our foibles and our idiosyncrasies. When we accept what we feel, then we can slowly make our way towards a firm decision to claim our own good self: body and spirit, one unique spark of the divine.

WHEN WE TRULY SENSE WHAT WE ARE DOING, THAT'S WHEN WE HAVE A CHOICE, THAT'S WHERE CHANGE TAKES PLACE.

Sandra Bain Cushman

Accept What You Feel, Then Decide to Feel Good

- *Read completely through these directions. Then do the exercise.* Close your eyes. By slowly and calmly breathing deeply, let your body relax. Starting with your feet, relax each part of your body. If you need to stretch, do so. After your feet, focus your attention on your legs, letting them relax, and so on, until you have relaxed your whole body. Take your time. Next, focus your attention on each individual part of your body. Starting with your feet; just notice any feelings. Get in touch with how you are experiencing your body right now. Make a slow inner tour of your body from bottom to top. When you have finished, write down any feelings. Note any resistance. Ask yourself: What do I feel about my body?

- *We recommend that you stand before a full-length mirror to do this exercise—unclothed is best.* Complete the systematic relaxation (described in the previous exercise), eyes open, starting with your feet and finishing with your neck and face. Next, focus your attention on one part or aspect of your body that you feel most dislike for, discomfort with, embarrassment about. Look at that part of you. Just be aware of your feelings. Ask yourself: What is it that most bothers me about this part of myself? Where did these feelings come from? Next, take a seat (still unclothed) and write a dialogue between you and the body part. If you feel silly doing this, just remember that no one is watching, so go ahead and try it. Begin the dialogue by asking the part or aspect of your body some question. Write down what your body says. As you continue the discussion you might have some interesting revelations. End your dialogue by thanking and affirming the body part for all that it does in your life. Remember: You are the one to decide to affirm or continue feeling negative.

- The German mystic Meister Eckhart once said, "If the only prayer you say in your entire life is 'Thank You,' that would suffice." Here's an exercise in thanking your body for its goodness. Again, stand, lie down, or sit in front of a mirror. Choose to feel good about your bodyself. Thank and affirm each part of your body. If negative messages try to crowd in, just let them pass through your body and out. Concentrate on thankfulness and affirmations. Look intently at whatever body part for which you are giving thanks. Here are two examples:

- "Skin, thank you. You protect me and let me feel the cool breeze and cat's fur."

- "Bones and muscles, thanks. You help me walk towards people I love and also enable me to work."

Continue to thank and affirm each part of your body, inside and outside.

THE REWARD FOR ATTENTION IS
ALWAYS HEALING.

Julia Cameron

Our Perfect Bodies

Ann Symonds tells the story about her trips to the swimming pool and the feelings she encounters there. In being open to these feelings, acceptance, even joy, about her bodyself unfolds.

For more than twenty years, I've been a regular at a local high school's indoor swimming pool. The pool is the right length and temperature for lap swimming, but the women's locker room leaves something to be desired. The changing area is no more than a cinder block cell, with cement floors, ceiling-high casement windows and a wall of rusty lockers.

Four nights a week I shed my clothes in these Spartan surroundings, lending sympathetic looks to newcomers despairing over the drafty windows and open showers. We have no choice but to undress, shower, and dress in full view of one another. Our only chance for privacy is behind the closed door of a toilet stall. Despite the lack of health club comforts, I've never been willing to give up the convenience of swimming at a pool a mile from my house. Now I'm realizing that convenience isn't the only benefit: dressing and undressing in front of naked women all these years has gradually helped me accept my body.

When I was in my early twenties, I thought my breasts were too small, my waist too wide and my hips too chunky. I set out to change my dimensions. But when I dieted to slenderize my hips, my breasts shrank too. I learned the hard way that there is little I can do to significantly alter what I've been given. By then I was out of college and away from gym class—the only place I'd been accustomed to seeing naked women. The only bare bodies I saw were on the movie screen. Not surprisingly, these movie images increased my self-doubt. Thanks to imaginative lighting and well-chosen poses, the actresses and models appeared perfect: endowed with abundant breasts, narrow waists, slightly curving hips and smooth skin.

In the throes of my despair, I began searching for a place to swim. That's when I found the community pool. At first I was embarrassed to undress in front of others, but as I got used to the exposure, I paid less attention to myself and began to notice the women around me.

For the first time, I appreciated the beauty of the female body in all its variety. Over the course of many nights I saw a very pregnant woman with a bulging stomach and deep, dark areaolae; an elderly woman with a stooped back, sagging skin and folds of flesh draping her midriff; a flat-chested little girl in her birthday suit; a twentysomething beauty with perfect breasts and slender hips; and me—in my mid forties, slim, with hard, visible stomach muscles, no waistline, and meager breasts.

Fat women, skinny women, old women, young women. It was beauty borne of nature, not perfection. Each night I marveled at our different shapes and sizes.

I watched regular patrons—whom I know by sight, not by name—grow round with pregnancy, gain or lose weight, turn gray and acquire wrinkles. I saw breasts scarred by surgery, wounds long since healed, and the stump of an amputated leg. Ever so gradually I became comfortable with the wide variety of female anatomy and the changes it undergoes with pride or indifference. I realized the absurdity of my dream for perfection. Beauty is everywhere if we just look for it.

A number of years ago, an acquaintance visited me while on a business trip. Before she arrived, I conjured her face in my mind and felt a twinge of pity for her because of her unattractive features. By classical standards, her nose is too wide, her face too flat, and her complexion too sallow. Sure enough, my memory was confirmed when she knocked at my door. Then she spoke. And everything changed. Her face lit up and she released a radiant energy. I saw why people were drawn to her. She exuded beauty in a way others who have achieved mere physical perfection rarely do.

After she left, I was ashamed of myself for focusing on her lack of so-called beauty. And although that incident occurred almost a decade ago, its lesson remains close to my conscience. Each night I watch the women at the pool and am reminded again of how beauty comes in many shapes and sizes. But perhaps most important, it comes from within.

Ann Symonds

WE HAVE THE BODY WE HAVE
BECAUSE IT IS PRECISELY THE VEHI-
CLE IN WHICH WE CAN BEST DO
WHAT WE CAME TO DO.

Christiane Northrup

"I'm No Susan Sarandon"

On my way out of the supermarket the other day I noticed a poster of actress Susan Sarandon plastered on the wall of the store's video rental section. She is breathtaking. Not gussied-up glamorous or moviestar gorgeous, mind you, just simply beautiful.

"Someday," I thought. "Someday, I'll be beautiful, too."

And why not? After all, Sarandon is not much older than me, and she, too, is the mother of young children. I'm thinking all this as I make my way to the parking lot, carrying a gallon of skim milk, some Pop Tarts, a couple of packs of toilet paper, and a box of tissues.

I have to laugh at myself.

I seem to harbor the belief that if I'm patient, then someday it will be my turn to be beautiful. That if I brush my teeth, wash my face, make the beds, make breakfast, walk the dog, feed the cat, take care of business, and don't complain too much, then someday. . . .

Well, I'm forty-one years old. And I think it's time I stopped dreaming.

Please understand. It's not that I'm hideous or anything. Actually, I would guess that I'm fairly averagelooking. In fact, the two most important men in my life—my wonderful husband and my sweet fouryear-old son—think that I'm a total babe.

But stop-'em-dead-in-their-tracks gorgeous? Well, it certainly does seem like something every woman should get a shot at. But I'm smart enough to realize that a little nip here and a little tuck and pull there won't give me the face of Christie Brinkley, Candice Bergen or, sadly, even the lovely Susan Sarandon.

Still feeling a bit left out and sort of wistful, I lace up my sneakers and go to a step aerobics class. The instructor of this particular class has a really fabulous body, but she's not especially pretty. Rather plain, in fact. But she seems utterly content with herself, chattering on and on about the minutiae of her life in between calling out the counts for "repeaters," "side leg lifts," and "step squats."

So I step and sweat and sweat and step for forty-five grueling minutes, and it's not until the class is finally over and I'm lying on the floor stretching and trying to catch my breath that I have the energy to take a good look at the other women working out around me.

Directly in front of me is a lady in her forties, I'd say, but it's a bit hard to tell. I first notice her breasts. We're about the same size, except that when she lies down on her back to do abdominal crunches her breasts stay up. Mine—what's left of them after they've been squashed flat like two pancakes by my uncomfortable sports bra—fall to the side, aiming for the floor, like just about everything else on my body.

But then I notice a very tiny scar behind the woman's right ear, and I wonder if that explains the perpetually astonished expression on her taut face. And her skin is remarkably smooth. Is it the work of a plastic surgeon, I wonder? Her legs are tan, but closer inspection reveals that the tan is from a bottle. Clearly, she's working very hard at being beautiful.

Then there's the young woman sitting directly behind me. Barely into her twenties, she's all skin and bones, her elbows jut out like wooden clothes hangers.

She has the kind of waspy good looks that most women her age covet, but her face is washed out and pale, too thin and worried-looking. And she's also not sweating, thank God. She's so thin, if she were to sweat—even a little bit—she might just disappear altogether.

Then I turn and look at myself in the mirror. I don't see Susan Sarandon's beautiful face gazing back at me but my own, caked with sweat and flushed with effort.

I feel pretty good.

Barbara Matson

CHANGE OCCURS WHEN ONE BECOMES WHAT SHE IS, NOT WHEN SHE TRIES TO BECOME WHAT SHE IS NOT.

Ruth P. Freedman

WAY 5:

Celebrate Your Senses!

SMELLS, ARE SURER THAN SOUNDS

AND SIGHTS

TO MAKE YOUR HEARTSTRINGS

CRACK.

Rudyard Kipling

I had just moved to La Crosse, Wisconsin, a Mississippi River city with a population of about 50,000. A retreat center had asked me to do a program for them, so I was meeting the director to arrange the event. I pulled up in front of the imposing, red brick building that had once housed novices for the community. I had seen institutions like it many times, and expected it to be "convent clean." What I had not expected was what happened next.

Entering the front door, a fragrance assailed my nose, flooding me with memories of the elementary school I had attended thirty years before in Memphis. The smells of chalk dust, fresh floor wax, and old books mixed into a combination that mesmerized me and carried me back to the hot August days when I would walk the couple of blocks to my grammar school to pound erasers clean, move desks, and straighten books for the principal. Once again, the pleasure of smelling stunned me with its power.

A person with a good sense of smell can identify around ten thousand odors. And of course, a good sniffer incredibly enhances our sense of taste. The sharp bite of cilantro or the sweetness of chocolate nearly vanish when our noses are stuffy. Each smell harbors memories and emotions. Do you remember your childhood whenever the fragrance of chocolate chip cookies assails your nose? Do you glance around for a long-lost friend when the smell of the perfume she always wore wafts into your nostrils?

Our nose is not the only sense we tend to take for granted. Many of us ignore our senses until something goes wrong with one of them. But we can decide to celebrate our senses by enjoying them. Much of this enjoyment stems from simply paying attention to what we are seeing, touching, smelling, tasting, and hearing.

By celebrating our senses, we come to love our bodyself even more, and all of life becomes much more full. In *Pilgrim at Tinker Creek,* Annie Dillard says about seeing:

> Beauty and grace are performed whether or not we will or sense them. The least we can do is try to be there. . . . We must somehow take a wider view, look at the whole landscape, really see it, and describe what's going on there. Then we can at least wail the right questions into the swaddling band of darkness, or, if it comes to that, choir the proper praise.

Our senses are like good friendships that only get better when we pay attention to them, enjoy them, spend time with them, and embrace them.

THOSE WHO ALLOW THEIR DAYS TO
PASS BY WITHOUT PRACTICING GEN-
EROSITY AND ENJOYING LIFE'S
PLEASURES ARE LIKE A BLACK-
SMITH'S BELLOWS; THEY BREATHE,
BUT DO NOT LIVE.

Sanskrit proverb

Celebrate Your Senses!

- Lie down on the floor. Close your eyes. Breathe slowly and deeply for a few minutes. Then focus your attention on the sensations where your body is touching the floor: your heels, calves, thighs, buttocks, back, arms, and head. How does the floor feel? Hard or soft? Cool or warm? Be open to all the subtle differences of feeling. Then turn on your side or front. Notice the parts of your body touching the floor. Focus again on the sensations you are experiencing.

- Go for a walk outdoors. Pay attention to the sensations that you feel on your skin, in your nose and ears. Like Annie Dillard, "be there . . . take a wider view, look at the whole landscape, really see it." How do these sensations make you feel all over? Conclude your walk by offering "the proper praise."

- Eyes closed, smell the odors around you. Try to pick out the source of each one. Then go into your kitchen and smell spices, baked goods, fruits, vegetables, and so on. Smell the skin on your arm. Go elsewhere in your home: smell. Take your time, savor each fragrance, and be thankful for your nose.

- Try these seeing exercises:
  - Gaze at the night sky, especially on a starlit or moonlit night.

    Relax, breathe deeply, and see.
  - Remember when you were a child lying on your back watching the clouds glide by? Take your inner child outside to a grassy spot; get comfortable. Watch the clouds sail by.
  - Spend an enjoyable time people-watching. Pay attention to the wondrous variety and beauty.
- Resolve to find at least one way to celebrate your senses each day.

GOD IS EVERYTHING WHICH IS
GOOD, AS I SEE, AND THE GOOD-
NESS WHICH EVERYTHING HAS IS
GOD.

Julian of Norwich

Stop and Smell the Crayons (Walking With a Five-Year-Old)

Sometimes we learn to celebrate our senses when we allow ourselves to be tutored by children who have not yet learned to turn off the pleasures of seeing, tasting, touching, smelling, and hearing. They may also teach us to slow down enough to be in touch.

I walk for exercise. Every evening, I try to squeeze in a brisk one- to three-mile hike, usually up and down my neighborhood streets. The other day, my five-year-old begged to join me. At first I resisted. I knew his little legs couldn't keep pace with mine and that I wouldn't burn off as many calories as I'd planned. But he looked so hopeful, and had asked so nicely (for a change) that I gave in. "Okay," I sighed, mildly annoyed.

Sure enough, we hadn't gone past three houses when we had to stop to sniff some honeysuckle. We watched a cat climb on a roof. We chased a squirrel, picked up a ladybug, counted birds on a telephone wire, collected pinecones, watched dandelion seeds float on the breeze. We traced letters that had been formed by cracks in the road. We read the street signs ("S-T-O-P"). And we held hands.

My pulse rate barely registered above resting—but it felt great. Instead of just pumping my legs while mulling a mile-long to-do list as the scenery whizzed by me unacknowledged, I learned to walk the way a five-year-old does: with my whole body and all of my senses thinking of nothing but the pleasure of the here-and-now.

Opportunities to stop and savor my children often seem as rare as unspilled juice cups. Between molding manners, wiping noses, cleaning up messes, and reminding them not to run into the street, I'm often too busy being a mom to enjoy being a mom. I'd like to think that my son will always remember me as the mother I was on our walk: patient, attentive, exploratory, loving, fun. Or will he recall only the blur of the warp-speed model who hustles him through his bath and bedtime routines so I can finish up 10,000 little tasks before I turn in? "Hurry up!" I find myself saying, all too often. "We're late!"

Sometimes I truly have to rush. But more often I suspect I'm rushing out of habit, a grinding, relentless, grownup drone that dictates I ought to be doing something constructive every minute of the day. I'm so entrenched in our fast-food, e-mail, drive-through culture that I risk speeding past the slow-motion magic right under my nose. I forget all the snuggly reasons that I wanted children in the first place.

Sure, kids are an enormous accelerating factor in parents' lives—if you're not tending to their morals and their self-esteem, it's laundry and meals, play dates and carpools, homework and ballgames. Easily overlooked in the necessary hubbub is the fact that children are also a wonderful excuse for decelerating.

Swinging on playground swings. Building a snowman. Tinkering with a model car. Watching cartoons in pj's on Saturday morning. Eating bowls of cold cereal. If you've ever watched a three-year-old make a single Oreo last for twenty minutes, you've seen this pleasure Zen in action.

The realization that children have plenty to teach their parents—if we slow down long enough to let them—first dawned on me the Christmas my son, Henry, was two and a half. Eyeing the mound of packages under the brightly-lit tree, I felt the familiar "whadja-get" giddiness pulsing through my veins. But after opening each gift, he did something surprising: He played with it. On and on, not giving a thought to anything else until he was through enjoying each car, book, or ball. When he opened the video *Christmas Eve on Sesame Street*, his gift opening came to a standstill for thirty minutes while he watched it. He was still opening gifts the next morning. And why not?

So yesterday, when my two preschoolers hauled out a tin of crayons and paper, I resisted the impulse to simultaneously read the newspaper, fix dinner, and make a phone call while they were preoccupied. Instead, I got down on the floor with them. Forest green. Robin's egg blue. Even the colors' names were relaxing. We drew flowers, spider-webs, and countless rainbows. They were delighted, and so was I. An hour sped by

before I got a crick in my knee from lying on the floor.
I stood up. C'mon, guys, let's go for a walk.

Paula Spencer

AWARENESS, IN AND OF ITSELF, IS
CURATIVE.

Robert Marrone

TOUCHING IS NOURISHMENT.

Gay Luce

The Healing Touch of a Generous Woman

While recovering from cancer treatment, Marilyn Greenberg learned that all the delightful sensations of receiving makeup can be healing, particularly when given by people who care.

I was attending a program for cancer patients called "Look Good, Feel Better." That sense of this-can't-be-me, which had washed over me when I first heard the diagnosis of cancer, was swamping me again. Why was I here? To try on makeup? I had long looked down my unpowdered nose at cosmetics. Possessing simple good health, I'd remained my old-fashioned mother's old-fashioned daughter, scorning powder and paint. Now everything had changed: I had cancer. My surgical scars were new, my pallor, my outlook.

And so here I was, along with fourteen other women, all cancer patients, gathering in the hospital recreation room. Some of us were outpatients, others shuffled in pushing IV poles or were brought in with the assistance of a nurse. But however we arrived, whatever our mobility, you could see our illness in our faces, and our anxiety. With weeks or months of treatment behind us—drug trials, medical protocols of various descriptions—we had all learned to be apprehensive.

The recreation room was spacious and sunny. Groups of thick-leafed plants, with an occasional blooming, leggy orchid sticking its head up through the foliage, grew in pots and window boxes. Patients in gowns and robes sat at tables playing cards, working jigsaw puzzles, or companionably chatting with one another. Besides the IVs, there wasn't one piece of medical equipment in sight. In this cheerful atmosphere we began to relax.

Four beautifully groomed and tranquil volunteers welcomed us to the program. Lynn, Gail, Renee, and Marguerite invited us to rest awhile from our preoccupation with tests and treatments, to take a break and give ourselves over, at least temporarily, to a sense of play and pleasure. These women come to the hospital every week, often straight from their jobs, just for the sake of others.

Each of us received as gifts an array of cosmetics from well-known companies that donate their products to the program. I looked at the eyeliner, highlighter, and foundation in my hands. It was all news to me. But it didn't matter that I was a novice when it came to these everyday tools for most women. Our volunteers knew what they were about. Over the next hour, beneath their gentle fingers, new faces began to emerge, mine among them. Sparse eyebrows were delicately feathered in. Cheeks blushed, and lips bloomed. Sallow became rosy, and olive became rich. A few eyelashes were made to do the work of many with just the right whisper of mascara.

Our volunteers put themselves at the service of every skin color, every problem, each blotch or dry patch. Laughing at little things, making conversation, exchanging bottles and brushes with each other, they never flinched—even when, as in my case, the hair they brushed came off in their hands.

Having cancer is hard. Sometimes the treatment can seem harder. But when, at the end of the hour, I looked in the mirror, what I saw was not just color or contour, but hope. Looking good had made me feel better, after all.

It wasn't only the makeup that had raised my spirits. Equally important were the women who'd applied it. They had reminded me of something I'd almost forgotten.

Were you lucky enough to have a grandmother who smoothed your hair back from your brow when you had a fever? Did your mother soothe your skinned knees with her cool fingers? Are you one of the fortunate, with true women friends to take you by the hand and help you back to the world again if you should need it? Then you will know what I mean when I say that Gail, Renee, Lynn, and Marguerite, in that one hour, taught me again what I had always known, but lost sight of for a while: There is healing and comfort in the simple touch of a generous woman.

Marilyn Greenberg

HANDS ARE THE HEART'S LANDSCAPE.

John Paul II

OFTEN THE HANDS WILL SOLVE A MYSTERY THAT THE INTELLECT HAS STRUGGLED WITH IN VAIN.

Carl Jung

Eat, Drink, Enjoy

EATING IS LIFE. . . . WITH EVERY MORSEL OF FOOD SWALLOWED A VOICE WITHIN SAYS, "I CHOOSE LIFE."

Marc David

Several years ago, Joyce and I sang with a large chorus, performing Carl Orff's *Carmina Burana* with a local symphony for the spring concert. I needed to rent a tuxedo jacket. When I called one of the two rental stores, the conversation took an unexpected twist.

"I need a tux jacket for three performances," I told the clerk.

"Sure, we can do that. What size?"

"Well, my suit is a size 54 portly."

"Sorry, *porkly* don't come in that size."

At first I thought the clerk was joking, so I asked. "So you don't have 54 portly?" I said "portly" slowly, deliberately.

Without even the suggestion of a snicker, the clerk replied, "No, we don't have porkly until size 60. Hell, a guy from one of the casinos came in here asking for a size 70 porkly. Can you imagine that!"

A size 70 was hard for even a big guy like me to imagine. At this point, I had a laughing attack. I guessed that porkly described me better than portly anyway.

This conversation prompted two things: first, I was relieved to find out once again that some behemoths bigger than I was really walked the planet. Second, in our fifth decade of life, our bodies were beginning to tire of extra pounds. So, Joyce and I decided that, out of love for our bodyselves, we had best make some changes. We were both just a bit too porkly.

We realized that what we really had to do was learn to eat well. Our Teutonic genes leaned us towards the porkly; our own habits of eating didn't help. We needed a whole new spirituality of eating. Where to start? We went back to basics.

Basic No. 1: We had to embrace food as a friend. Food is not the enemy. It is created to be enjoyed, relished, cherished. In his novel *Look Homeward, Angel*, Thomas Wolfe's description gives proper reverence to the glory of food:

> [The family] fed stupendously. . . . In the autumn, they barreled huge frosty apples in the cellar. . . . Smoked bacons hung in the pantry, the great bins were full of flour, the dark recessed shelves groaned with preserved cherries, peaches, plums, quinces, apples, pears. . . .
>
> In the morning they rose in a house pungent with breakfast cookery, and they sat at a smoking table loaded with brains and eggs, ham, hot biscuit, fried apples seething in their gummed syrups, honey, golden butter, fried steak, scalding coffee. Or there were battercakes, rum-colored molasses, fragrant brown

sausages, a bowl of wet cherries, plums, fat juicy bacon, jams.

Basic No. 2: We needed to have more quality time with our friend food, but less quantity. A story is told about the Spanish mystic, Teresa of Avila, who lived in the sixteenth century. One day a friend donated some partridges to the convent. Teresa ordered them cooked for supper. When Teresa sat down and began eating the partridges with obvious gusto, a visitor, expecting her to be more abstemious, criticized her. Looking up from her plate, Teresa said, "When I pray, I pray, and when I partridge, I partridge."

Like Teresa, we tried to make sure that whatever we prepared to eat tickled our taste buds, was nourishing, and that we consumed it reverently and attentively. In other words, when we ate, we ate. We didn't read the morning paper, watch TV, or plan how we were going to paint the house.

Basic No. 3: If we wanted to make food a friend, we needed to learn more about it. We started reading about food. We checked ingredients. We searched the web for a few good food sites. Like our friends, food has surprises and huge variety.

Basic No. 4: Food became an opportunity for thanksgiving and celebration. This seems natural, but we tended to eat so fast that we seldom reverenced the time of eating and drinking. Stories of feasting fill the Bible. Key moments in the life of Jesus happened at meals: feeding of thousands with only a few loaves and fish, the wedding feast at Cana, and the Last Supper. Islam's holy book, the Koran, pictures heaven as a feast: those in the "gardens of delight" shall be fed "with such fruits as shall please them best, and with flesh of such birds, as they shall long for." And so, we asked, why not choose to make each meal a small celebration, a taste of heaven with our friends, food, and drink?

Our body needs food to live and thrive. We need to make friends of food and drink if we are to love our bodies. Ironically, if we embrace food and drink as friends, they cease being enemies of our waistlines and become partners in life's celebration.

TRUE HAPPINESS LIES IN EATING AND DRINKING AND ENJOYING WHATEVER HAS BEEN ACHIEVED UNDER THE SUN, THROUGHOUT THE LIFE GIVEN BY GOD: FOR THIS IS THE LOT OF HUMANITY!

Book of Ecclesiasticus

Eat, Drink, Enjoy

- Keep a log of your eating and drinking habits for a week. Note what you ate and how long your meal took. How did eating feel? Are you having quality time with food and drink? At the end of the week, ponder these questions: Am I embracing food and drink as friends? Do I substitute quantity for quality of experience? Do I eat a balanced diet? Are my patterns of eating and drinking good for my body?

- At some time every day, try to eat something slowly and deliberately, focusing all of your attention on just eating. We recommend fruit or raw vegetables. For example, if you are eating an orange, peel it slowly, smell the fragrance, feel the spray of the juice. Eat each slice one by one, rolling the slice in your mouth, consciously biting down, chewing slowly. In short, turn eating one thing into a daily meditation. This way food becomes an act of thankfulness, awareness, and pleasure. Besides, one common piece of advice for those reforming their eating is to do it more slowly.

- Buy a cookbook filled with new, healthy recipes. Try new dishes, new tastes. Make eating and drinking a celebration.

IT SEEMS TO ME THAT OUR THREE BASIC NEEDS, FOR FOOD AND SECURITY AND LOVE, ARE SO ENTWINED THAT WE CANNOT THINK OF ONE WITHOUT THE OTHER.

M.F.K. Fisher

Abundance

Anne Hooper was a good cook. Everyone thought so, and an invitation to her table was one to be cherished. She wasn't a gourmet cook. Nothing exotic, although she did scour magazines and cookbooks for new recipes. She stuck to meat-and-potatoes kind of recipes, primarily because her husband liked the basics. Also, setting a proper table, the presentation of food, was important to Anne, especially when having guests. Anne Hooper was my mother, and I grew up watching and absorbing the whole ritual of creating a feast for her family and friends.

My parents entertained a lot. Mother loved putting on dinner parties, and they were always elegant events. They nourished the eyes as well as the stomach, and my mother was always a charming hostess. The table was covered with a linen tablecloth, the quality improving through the years. The silver flatware and dishes sparkled in the candlelight, and the crystal glasses sang when I would tap them with a fork. The clear china had a silver rim, coordinating with the silverware.

As a little girl I would help my mother set the table, being particularly careful not to drop anything and to check for any water spots on the glasses or silver. As we worked, the house would slowly fill with the aromas coming from the kitchen. Bread baking. A pie or cake for dessert. The heat from the oven preparing a warm welcome for our guests. All this in preparation for the main event.

Our table guests usually included at least one priest from the parish or a couple of nuns, along with other friends of the family. Often my brother, a priest, would bring friends from the school where he taught. We would begin with grace. Mother would ask someone to say the blessing, or she would bow her head and pray, "Bless us, O Lord, and these thy gifts, which we are about to receive from thy bounty. Through Christ, our Lord. Amen."

We would begin with an appetizer, usually shrimp cocktail. In the early days, Mom would use a fluted glass to hold the shrimp and cocktail sauce. Later she presented special dishes sitting on crushed ice. Always accompanied by Ritz crackers. The mixed green salad with French dressing would be on the side.

Then would come the entrée with the accompanying potato and vegetable dishes. An image I compared this to is of those grand banquets when the double doors open and the servants begin the procession of food to grand music. At our banquets, my mother would appear at the door of her small kitchen looking a bit frenetic, perspiration on her forehead, hurrying to get all the food on at one time so none cooled off. There would be the china platter of roast beef or slices of Chateaubriand. At least two potatoes, white and sweet. And corn and peas or mixed vegetables or beans. As soon as the serving dishes were put on the table, Mother would take her place at the head, surveying to make sure she had not forgotten anything, saying with a sigh, "Please, begin." She would then watch that everyone took at least one helping of each dish.

The inevitable, "Anne, this is wonderful!" or "Mrs. Hooper, can I have some more?" brought a smile of contentment to her face. And she would press everyone to take another helping, for she always made enough for multiple meals. Apple pie, truffle, or pineapple upside-down cake with coffee completed the meal.

We didn't have an easy life as I was growing up because of illnesses of both my mom and my dad. However, these gatherings around the table with the food, presentation, and the charm of my mother were a bit of a respite when Mom would feed our bodies and nurture our spirits. Her pleasure at creating the right sauces and baking the special dessert added to the experience of her nurturing of whomever was at the table that night. Having a bountiful table was Mother's gift to us, an expression of love to her husband and children and friends.

For the last Christmas we had with Mom, we had taken her home from the hospital. The left side of her body was weakened from a brain tumor. In September, she had dreamed of being alive at Christmas and having the house filled with the tree and the aromas of holiday cooking. I was determined we would have that Christmas.

My brother and dad brought back a huge Christmas tree. Under my mother's halting direction, I attempted to cook the Christmas dinner. My brother and I set the table with the Belgium linen tablecloth and shining silver. I cooked the vegetables, the potatoes, and the Chateaubriand. Unfortunately, my cheese sauce curdled, but I served it anyway.

There were just the four of us, my mother, my father, my brother, and me. We prayed that God would walk with us through this journey. Mother prayed that she would have ten more years to live. And then we began to eat the vegetables, potatoes, and meat with the curdled cheese sauce. Not up to Mother's standards, but for a few short minutes we were together, receiving through my inadequate hands the gift of Mother's love and also her legacy of nurturing.

Over the years, I have developed a love/hate relationship with food. I haven't had the patience my mother had, and I have seen food as the enemy of my waistline. But I'm coming to realize that the offering of food—even to myself—is a gift that represents the love and abundance of the Spirit. If Mother had lived these past many years, her cooking may have taken a more healthy turn, less beef and low fat. However, her home would still be filled with the warmth of the oven, and her table would abound with the aromas and colors and savory tastes of the meal prepared with love.

Rosalie Hooper-Thomas

THINK FOR A MOMENT ABOUT THE HOLINESS OF OUR OWN FOOD, AND THE WAYS THAT COOKING AND SHARING A MEAL CAN BE FORMS OF LOVE AND PRAYER.

Brian Doyle

Uncle Marvin's Barbecue

Enjoying food not only nourishes our body, but also can be a source of community, celebration, and fond memory.

M y Aunt Mitzi wanted Uncle Marvin's barbecue recipe. She had desired it for years. These two loved each other, no doubt there, but his secrecy about the ingredients to his sauce drove her to distraction. His staunch refusal to give it to her had caused, years before, the only fight any of us ever witnessed between them.

Now Marvin's gnarled hands lay quietly on the sheets of his hospital bed. He had so many things wrong with him that he just told visitors that he was dying of the "allovers." Mitzi stayed at the hospital day and night. She had lost one husband, now her second love stood before eternity's portal.

"Marvin, you're going any time. So it's time to tell me about the barbecue sauce." Mitzi stood over his bed. A stoical sort, her voice was steady but without edge to it.

"Damn. Here I'm dyin' and all you can think over is that sauce. Woman, you been after me for years for that. Well, I've a mind to just die and leave you stewing over it." His eyes twinkled. He looked over at me and, when Mitzi got distracted, he winked.

Marvin grew up in a sharecropper's family in east Arkansas. He didn't have much education, but he knew the essence of barbecue. Indeed, if anyone gave doctorates in sauce, he would have graduated *magna cum laude*.

Every Sunday afternoon when I was a kid, most of the Werner clan showed up at my grandmother's house. My mother always guilt-tripped us into going by saying, "Your grandmother's old. She's going to pass on any time, so you want to visit her while you can." This worked even in our high school years. (In fact, Granny lived to be ninety-five and died when I was twenty-nine and wandering around Europe. She had eaten a big plate of spaghetti and put away a beer for supper. The next morning my aunt found her still in bed long after she usually got up. She died with a slight smile on her face or so my aunt said. Granny loved her

spaghetti and a cold beer. She might have had a broad-
er smile if her last meal had been Marvin's barbecue.)

The fact is that I only made the weakest of arguments about visiting on Sundays because every so often
Marvin would be cooking his barbecue for the family.
We could never predict when, so we went every week,
dreading a missed opportunity.

He would start the coals early in the morning in his
half-barrel grill. Then he would go to the eight o'clock
church service. By the time he returned the coals would
be nearly ready. After changing out of his church
clothes, he would sequester himself in the kitchen and
brew his sauce. We knew it had onions, fresh lemon,
Tabasco sauce, vinegar, and so on, but he guarded the
mixture like a state secret. Everyone in the family tried
to duplicate the sauce, but no one came close.

Then Marvin would seat himself in a lawn chair
with his Old Crow highball close at hand. The rest of
the day was spent turning the chicken, brushing on his
sauce, monitoring the coals, and telling stories to who-
ever sat down in the other two nearby lawn chairs.
Given the size of our clan, the magnetism of the fragrance coming out of the grill, and Marvin's gentle
good humor, the two chairs never emptied for long.
Back in the kitchen, Aunt Mitzi and some of the other
aunts would be making coleslaw and potato salad.

By four o'clock hunger had exhausted all of us kids.
Most of the adults had been mellowed by a Blue
Ribbon or a highball. We looked hungrily out to see if
Marvin was ready to feed us. With a slight wave of the
hand, he would signal for my aunt to let us fix our
plates. First Aunt Mitzi fixed Granny's plate. Marvin
would search through the chicken to find some choice
piece for her. Then each of us kids held out our plate to
him, knowing that no matter what piece we got, it
would be delicious.

Eating commenced in virtual silence, and always
we ate the chicken first. The taste defies description:

husky smoke from the charcoal, tart lemon softened by tomato, a hint of fire from the Tabasco. I have made pilgrimage to famous barbecue joints from Memphis to Atlanta, Dallas to New Orleans, but no barbecue ever matched Marvin's.

Now Marvin had only days to live.

Sotto voce my cousins and I—now in our late thirties—stood out in the waiting room wondering if Mitzi would finally get Marvin to spill the beans. No one said anything to her, but we think she knew we were dying to know.

Finally, the day before he passed, Mitzi exited Marvin's room with a triumphant smile. Gathering us around her, she whispered two words, "Got it." We all breathed a sigh, not even aware that we had been holding our breath.

Some weeks later, we gathered at Mitzi's house. Word had spread that she was barbecuing. She followed the same ritual, except for the Old Crow highball. The fire seemed the same; the fragrance coming from Marvin's cooker seemed the same. As we had done as children, we lined up at four o'clock for our chicken.

Gathering reverently, we sat throughout the house. First one of us, then the rest began biting into our barbecued chicken. We chewed slowly, almost meditatively.

Then the looks started. Our glances at each other could only be described as a mixture of doubt, wonderment, disappointment, and humor. Something was missing. The barbecue was good, indeed very good, but without a doubt, some mysterious ingredient had been left out.

Mitzi looked around the room after finally tasting her chicken. A look of surprise, then fury mottled her face. "Damnit! Damnit!" She ripped off a few more swear words, then stopped, blushed, and then began helplessly laughing. We all knew that Marvin, a man who would give us the shirt off his back, had held on to one secret even to the grave.

None of us ever found out what he omitted. Some of us thought it might be a shot of Old Crow; others wondered if we just didn't have the coals right. Or we wondered if the ingredient missing was Marvin himself whose care, kindness, and gentle humor made the unique flavor that only he could add to the barbecue.

Eating with my family remains one of life's great pleasures. We've moved on to healthier meals as we've gotten older and more concerned about longevity, but what brought us together those many years ago was Uncle Marvin's barbecue.

Carl Koch

THE TABLE IS A MEETING PLACE, A GATHERING GROUND, THE SOURCE OF SUSTENANCE AND NOURISHMENT, FESTIVITY, SAFETY, AND SATISFACTION.

Laurie Colwin

THE SON OF MAN CAME, EATING AND DRINKING.

Gospel of Matthew

Go Ahead, Move, Dance, Walk, or Roll Along!

A LIVING BODY IS NOT A FIXED
THING BUT A FLOWING EVENT, LIKE
A FLAME OR A WHIRLPOOL.

Alan Watts

I was on my way to observe a new teacher at the high
school where I was an administrator, when I heard a
mixture of laughter, loud voices, and groans. Curious, I
headed towards the area from which the noises came. I
realized that the agitation emanated from Bob Cleary's
room, so I immediately relaxed. His classes often
seemed a bit chaotic. When I looked in, a burly linebacker was declaiming a poem by Longfellow. Over
near the chalkboard, a girl I had always thought shy
stood ready to write notes, summarizing the coming
discussion. As soon as the linebacker finished, Bob
opened the conversation. Hands shot up and the

83

discussion began. Knowing that all was as it should be, I proceeded on my way.

At lunch, I patrolled the cafeteria. Bob was easy to spot. Wherever he went, a little mob of students followed to ask questions, seek advice, pore out their woes, or organize the next student activity. As Student Activities Director, Bob kept up a hectic pace attending concerts, games, and dances.

Several years after I left the high school, the Board named him principal. This may not sound too special, but you see, Bob was a quadriplegic.

Even before I came there, I had heard tales of Bob Cleary: how he had been all set to attend the University of Illinois to become an architect, been paralyzed in a diving accident, and had languished at home until the U of I became accessible to people with disabilities. Bob took bachelor's and master's degrees in English, attended to by a loving sister. He finally landed a teaching job at the high school, got married, and now was a star teacher.

Working with Bob, I began to understand what courage, wit, hope, and faith were all about. Bob had minimal use of one arm, only enough to drive his wheelchair, but his face always moved, attending to people. His spirit was embracing of people.

Like many quadriplegics, Bob's body finally failed him. He died in his late forties, but he was still working with kids, still holding out hope for others to the time of his death. Now when I think about how we either move or die, I think of Bob. Alan Watts' remark "a living body is not a fixed thing but a flowing event, like a flame or a whirlpool," describes Bob. He was and is a flowing event, a flame that lights my soul. Bob moved through life, and lived through moving.

Living urges us to move: to journey from here to there, to stretch our bodies, to get up and go. Loving our body urges us to move, whether that means strolling along, rolling in a wheelchair, running, swimming, or playing fetch with our dog. Moving keeps our muscles toned and our minds ready. Moving affirms that we are living.

Even blindness need not be an obstacle to healthy moving. Triathlete Heidi Musser has been blind from birth. Yet at age thirty-three, she took a gold medal in the Triathlon World Championships. Connected by a tether to her coach and guide, she swam 1.5 kilometers, biked 40 kilometers, and ran 10 kilometers more. She remarked, "My blindness is not a hindrance, but an asset to success. My mother encouraged me to aim for my own inner strength. I hope to inspire disabled individuals worldwide to come out into the athletic arena for lots of fun."

Having survived cancer, Ardath Rodale of *Prevention* magazine fully appreciates moving too. She wrote:

> Each morning, as I take my early morning walk, I step into the sun. I am sure that I hear you saying, 'But sometimes the sky is filled with heavy clouds.' To me, the sunshine is in my mind and heart. I am a winner over cancer. The experience has taught me that each day is a special gift to be filled with joy and appreciation and love. To be healthy, I have learned to turn away from the shadow and face the sun. Perhaps you, too, have been faced with a challenge that has changed your life.
>
> Come with me as we open the door to take that morning walk. We are filled with anticipation of what we might find that's new. To hear the music of birds urges us to join their chorus. Their cheerfulness fills us with energy as we notice their busy activity, gathering food and building nests.

Moving helps us enjoy our body, feel its power, celebrate our surroundings, and of course grow healthier.

It's part of loving our bodyself, of letting the sunshine into all of our life.

THE BEST THING ANYBODY CAN DO

IS WALK.

Whoopi Goldberg

Go Ahead, Move, Dance, Walk, or Roll Along!

- Lean over slowly and pick up some object. Focus your attention on feeling the array of muscles as they contract and stretch. Then get down on all fours on the floor. Imagine that you are a cat. Arch your back, stretching all of your large back muscles. Then roll your head around like a cat does when it starts to unwind. Next, stretch your left leg out behind you as far as you can; and then repeat the process with your right leg. Arch your back again. Ponder all the muscles at work.

- Walk around your home barefoot. Notice all the textures of the flooring. Then, go for a walk outside— barefoot if you like. Pay close attention to the feel of your legs and feet. Feel the muscles pulling, your knees and joints bending. As each foot hits the ground, say "thanks." Jump up and down a couple of times. Do a spontaneous dance or move freely to some music. Celebrate your ability to move. If walking is a problem for you, the key here is to move whatever part(s) of your body can let you feel the power of muscles and nerves, bone and sinew working together.

- Pick at least one movement each day to really concentrate on. If you are peeling potatoes, peel potatoes and enjoy the movement. If you are eating spaghetti, attend to just eating, letting yourself celebrate this moment of movement. If you are typing at a keyboard, just type. Learn to be attentive to the wonder of your body's movement.

- Here is a simple plan for starting a regular regimen of walking: Week one, stroll at a comfortable pace for about ten minutes each day. The next week, increase the amount of time that you walk by one minute each day; work up to a brisk walk. During the next few weeks, try to aim at walking forty minutes each day at an energetic pace. Most important, enjoy the walk: think constructive thoughts, consider all the gifts you have been given, attend to the life around you.

- Resolve to move each day in some manner that stretches your body and opens your mind and heart. And if you feel hesitant, remember, "You can't steal second base and keep one foot on first."

MOVEMENT IS THE UNIFYING BOND

BETWEEN THE MIND AND THE BODY.

Deane Juhan

Dancing My Way Home

In the spring of 1993 I was in constant pain. Eighteen months earlier the car in which I was riding got rearended. After the accident spasms wracked my lower back and shooting pains ran from my right buttock down my leg into my foot, numbing my little toe. My neck ached all the time. The chronic pain and stiffness left my entire body tense. Sitting hurt. Lying down hurt. Standing hurt, although I experienced some relief if I swayed, shifting my weight from one foot to the other. Sometimes shaking one leg and then the other helped ease the pain. Careful swimming proved to be the only exercise I could do without undue pain. I was exhausted and depressed.

A friend suggested that I go with her to a retreat for women. Worried that pain would hamper my participation, I called one of the facilitators to explain my situation. She assured me that every activity would be completely optional. Tired of being tired and depressed, I decided to go.

At the end of the first session, Maria, a professional dancer, put on some music and began a delicate dance to bless the earth. Surprisingly, my feet started beating out the rhythm. Gradually, the other women joined the dance, each in her own way. Soon my whole body gently swayed to the pulse of the drum.

After the session, I realized that in those ten minutes of dancing, as I was completely absorbed in the music and movement, my pain had receded into the background. A bubble of happiness welled up in my chest.

Even so, lying in bed that night, the pain creeping inexorably back into my body, I marveled at myself. I had not danced for years. As a child I loved to dance and dreamed of becoming a dancer when I grew up. As my body filled out in adolescence, those dreams were swallowed up by self-consciousness. Later, when I gained weight in my thirties, dancing seemed unthinkable.

The next morning, when time came to go to the gym for movement, I grew nervous. Gyms always made me nervous. Then Maria dimmed the lights, put on some gentle music, and explained that we should simply listen to our bodies and move as we wished. There were no right or wrong movements. Maria encouraged us to close our eyes to help us focus within and keep us from worrying about what anyone else was doing. She invited us to feel our bones, our muscles, and our breath as we moved.

I started slowly, cautiously. Then as I relaxed, my body began to move without thought to the tones and rhythms of the music. My feet, arms, pelvis, spine came to life. I twirled in large looping circles. Tears streamed down my face. I was a little girl again. Back in my living room, at twilight. Dancing to the strings of Mantovani.

As I twirled, my body remembered the joy of dancing that had been dormant for thirty years. Gone was the fat that must not jiggle that had imprisoned me for so many years. Gone was the pain. I danced and wept with that heady mixture of joy and grief.

The rest of the retreat flew by like a pleasant dream. My back and leg pain came and went, but had eased overall. As I said goodbye to Maria, I realized that if it had not been for the pain I probably would have sat still for the whole weekend. Now I emerged as a dancer.

A few weeks after the retreat I joined a dance class for women led by Maria. Years later, I'm still dancing. I am usually the only fat woman there, but I seldom notice. Once the music begins, we're simply spirits in motion, pure energy, full of astonishing beauty.

Tonight, I put the finishing touches on my makeup, run a brush through my short brown hair touched with gray, don an elegant gown that slides fluidly down my body to the tops of my black dress pumps. The scoop-necked, long sleeve dress sparkles and shimmers. With my flowing rhinestone earrings and white feather boa, I'm ready to sing and dance in a cabaret fund-raiser for my church.

I am well into my forties, five feet eight inches tall, and well over 200 pounds, but I have trudged through a tunnel of pain to dance out the other end. I have found my way back into my body and into my spirit's dance.

Anne Peek

Think of the magic of that foot, comparatively small, upon which your whole weight rests. It's a miracle, and the dance . . . is a celebration of that miracle.

Martha Graham

Early Morning Offerings

Like many of us, Phyllis Theroux struggles to balance her professional life, which is more or less sedentary, and her need for physical activity. So she turned to walking, which not only became a time for exercise, but a time for spontaneous acts of kindness, a time to move body and soul.

It may not be everybody's story, but the struggle to lead a disciplined life is my constant battle. Being a writer, I fight with words. "No man ever regretted eating too little," says Thomas Jefferson on the door of my refrigerator. "You don't get good poetry by chatting with people," snaps Mexican poet Jaime Sabinas from the back of my telephone receiver. "The essential thing," says Albert Schweitzer on my office wall, "is that we strive to have light in ourselves."

Dr. Schweitzer's words hang above my desk as an extra source of inspiration. But if I leave my desk to spend more than a few minutes outside in the sun-soaked natural world, I am reluctant to go back into the house again. Conversely, after I have reaccustomed my eyes to the civilized interior trappings of lamps and furniture, the natural world begins to feel like so much raw material it is my obligation to stay inside and refine. In a way it is.

Every book in my library is an attempt by a man or woman to compress experience into a line of print. The paintings on my walls are each the result of somebody trying to extract the essence of what was actually seen and—with the motion of a brush—extend the vision. Human beings are always trying to take nature to another level, like the bits of driftwood I have turned into candlestick holders.

But six months ago I realized that, once again, the pendulum had swung too far toward the sedentary life, and unless I took myself to another level I would be in trouble. Buying a set of hand weights and a new pair of sneakers to spur me on, I became an early-morning walker. My goal was to get myself back into good phys-ical condition. My worry was that after a few weeks, or even days, of striding around the neighborhood I would get bored.

This is a small town. I already knew it like the back of my own hand, and I wasn't sure I would keep mov-ing if I didn't have a reason beyond my own health for doing it. Fortunately, I found one—delivering newspa-pers. Actually, I redeliver them. The route belongs to someone else who drives around town at 6 a.m., fling-ing newspapers out of her car window in front of peo-ple's houses. My unpaid, self-anointed job is to move them closer to the front door.

At first I simply hurled the papers up the walk, where they sometimes landed with a loud bang against the screen door. Then a strange thing happened. I began to regard each house the way one looks at the envelope one is about to address for a friend's Christmas card—with fondness. I upped my standards and started gently laying the paper on the mat.

I had not expected to take such a proprietary interest in my "customers," but soon I was beginning to notice everything with a more appreciative and observant eye—which porch had been repainted, which had just added dahlias to their day lilies. Every day I was less bored and more involved than the day before, wondering whether Ned Dillon was going to have to start staking his tomato plants or if Jody Aston, who only reads the newspapers on Sunday, even noticed that they were not lying in the dianthus anymore.

I am not, however, the only early-morning altruist. John and Becky Longmire use their walk up and down South Center Street to pick up trash. This is serious community service, whereas the walking I do around the community primarily serves me.

The Thompsons' hydrangea bush serves to remind me that it is an evil thing to steal flowers from someone else's garden, which further serves to remind me that it is my friend Pat's birthday. I alter my route to stick a sprig of wild hydrangea (from my own yard) between the rubber bands around her newspaper before I prop it against the front door.

"The search is on. . ." reads part of a headline through the yellow plastic cover. For what—a criminal, a lost child, a presidential candidate? Almost everybody on the block takes the paper. I stopped to dip my nose into the bowl of a magnolia blossom and wondered whether people who don't subscribe to newspapers don't care, or get their news on the World Wide Web, where one can hop around the virtual world like an angel. But the other morning, while putting one foot in front of the other in the real world, I felt a bit like an angel myself.

It was the day after the Irish had voted for political reunification. As I walked up to people's front doors with the local news, I listened on my portable radio to interviews of Irish and English men and women whose voices were as clear and seemingly as near as my own footsteps. A British journalist quoted Cato the Elder, an ancient Roman statesman, on the meaning of freedom. To be simultaneously delivering and receiving news in so many different places, time zones, and centuries pushed me to the brink of joy.

"Dakota," wrote Kathleen Norris in her book of the same name, "is the place where it all comes together. Surely this is one definition of sacred." Surely, as it all came together on that cool, mist-hung morning. Surely, as a magnolia flower, or a heart that did not know it had been closed, opens.

Surely.

Phyllis Theroux

SO THE LEGS ARE A LITTLE SHORT,
THE KNEES MAYBE KNOCK A LITTLE
BUT WHO LISTENS?

Gertrude Berg

W A Y   8 :

Take Some Time Every Day to Catch Your Breath

BREATH IS THE BRIDGE WHICH CON-
NECTS LIFE TO CONSCIOUSNESS. . . .
WHENEVER YOUR MIND BECOMES
SCATTERED, USE YOUR BREATH AS
THE MEANS TO TAKE HOLD OF YOUR
MIND AGAIN.

Thich Nhat Hanh

My friend Katie is a hero, at least to one of her students.

To save time and her meager budget, Katie and her speech team had brought their lunches along on their outing to the tournament. All the team members had dressed in their tournament clothes: boys wore sport coats, dress shirts, and ties; girls mostly wore dress slacks, nice blouses, and blazers. Their mood was upbeat. After all, they had won the last two tournaments against the best teams in the state.

Like kids everywhere, her team members dropped their speech team sophistication to compare lunches. The usual banter flew back and forth about who had baloney sandwiches and who had "healthy" stuff.

A concentrated quiet fell over the bus as the team ate. Katie recognized the hush as pre-tournament jitters.

Suddenly Chuck, her dramatic interp star, began grabbing for his throat. His eyes darted around frantically. The kids behind him started laughing. Chuck constantly played jokes.

Katie froze in her seat. When Chuck turned to the side, she saw his panicked look.

Rushing forward, she yanked him upright, tilted his head forward, grabbed him in a bear hug and, fist in his solar plexus, gave his chest a swift and strong pop. Nothing happened. The bus fell silent.

She jerked again. With a startled cough, Chuck hurled a hunk of roast beef out of his gaping mouth. The beef hit squarely in the middle of Jennifer's wrinkled forehead.

Chuck gasped for air. With an "Oh, yuck," Jennifer wiped her face.

Katie fell back into her seat and began weeping. The kids cheered.

Later at the tournament, the story circulated through the other teams. Katie blushed when nearly everyone congratulated her. On the ride back home, she thanked Dr. Heimlich, wherever he was. For weeks afterwards, Chuck would sheepishly kid her about having arms like a gorilla, then thank her again and admit, "I was really scared. I couldn't breathe. That's the last time I'll eat beef in a hurry."

It is easy to take breathing for granted: that is, until we can't catch it. Then, in the twinkling of an eye, we realize that unless we start breathing in moments, we'll die. Six to ten minutes without oxygen causes brain damage. Soon other organs experience damage and death. In short, no breath, no life.

Now most of us may never experience choking like Chuck, but we can consciously chose to be better breathers. Indeed, we often need to consciously catch our breath because the pace of our lives can be so harried that we may be slowly choking ourselves.

Stress, worry, and fear can literally take our breath away, not entirely, but significantly. Many of us spend much of our day taking short, shallow breaths. By the end of the day, we crash, exhausted. We find ourselves saying things like, "I didn't have a chance to breathe today, I was so busy." Or, "I just want to plop in front of the TV and catch my breath." Somehow our body knows what it needs: air.

Physically, emotionally, spiritually we need air. If we want to love our bodyself, we need air. With a total surface area nearly the size of a tennis court, our lungs have plenty of capacity to be nurtured by our breathing. Our lungs can then feed all of our cells hungry for oxygen.

Air is life. Deep breathing not only brings life to our bodyself, but deep, slow breathing sooths our fears and relieves our stress. So, we can love ourselves more by taking time each day for catching our breath.

THE BREATH IS THE CURRENT CONNECTING BODY AND MIND, CONNECTING US WITH OUR PARENTS AND OUR CHILDREN, CONNECTING OUR BODY WITH THE OUTER WORLD'S BODY. IT IS THE CURRENT OF LIFE.

Jon Kabat-Zinn

Take Some Time Every Day to Catch Your Breath

- Try to find short periods, even three or four minutes, every day to just breathe. You will be amazed at how refreshing these little breaks can be to body and spirit. Find a comfortable position; many people feel that they can breathe most readily sitting in a straight-backed chair. Then focus your attention on your own breathing. Breathe deeply and slowly so that your inflated lungs push out your abdomen. You can check this by putting your hands on your lower abdomen; feel your breath pushing your hands outward. Listen to your breath coming in slowly and steadily; listen to your breath flowing out. Your in-breaths and out-breaths should take about the same length of time. Focusing on your breathing can calm your mind. If a lot of thoughts distract you, just let them go and return to listening to your breath. At the end of your breath-catching time, stand up, stretch, smile, and continue with your daily activities.

- In several languages, the word for "breath" and the word for "spirit" are the same. According to the Christian Bible, Jesus is said to have breathed on his followers and said, "Receive the Holy Spirit." If you find this notion helpful, silently say the words, "Come, Spirit" in harmony with your deep breathing. Air and spirit connect us with all of life. So your deep breathing, "Come, Spirit" becomes a meditation and recognition of your unity with all of creation.

- Another way of "catching our breath" is to consider the cleanliness of the air we breathe. Pollution comes in many forms. Spend some time thinking about the air you breathe and what you might do to provide clean air for your lungs and those of other people. Ask yourself:

- Is my car tuned so that it runs cleanly? Do I use it more than I need to?

- Do I smoke? Do I inhale a lot of secondary smoke? If so, what can I do about this?

- What else might I do to insure clean air for myself and for others?

STUDENT, TELL ME, WHAT IS GOD?
HE IS THE BREATH INSIDE THE
BREATH.

Kabir

Good Thing You Had Your Seat Belt On

After a sabbatical in the mountains of New Mexico, I had returned to the Midwest refreshed and ready to resume my regular work. One thing that I had done for my health while in Santa Fe was to have a therapeutic massage once each month. It helped my circulation, relieved my aching back, and soothed my ruffled spirit. I was pleasantly surprised upon my return home to find that a fine massage therapist had just set up practice in La Crosse, a nearby city.

Usually scheduled for Friday afternoons, my massage became an exclamation point ending each month. Even the thirty-five mile drive along the banks of the Mississippi River became part of my welcomed ritual. This sunny day in October, the drive had been particularly delightful because the eagles were migrating. I watched out of the car's window as they glided in the air currents coming over the bluffs and off the water.

To reach La Crosse, Wisconsin, I had to take the bridge at La Crescent, Minnesota. The drive through this small town usually took five minutes. I had just slowed down in the 40 mile per hour speed zone when I saw a blue blur zip in front of me. I slammed on the brakes, skidded, and then crashed into the side of the Pontiac Grand Prix.

Stunned, shocked, pain spread across my chest. I couldn't breathe.

In what must have been seconds, people were yelling through the window, asking if I was okay. All I could do was nod. My legs and arms worked okay, so they weren't broken. Amazingly my glasses remained fixed on my nose. But my chest felt as if an elephant was stepping on it. Every small intake of air sent shock waves of pain throughout my torso.

The rescue squad and police managed to pull open the mangled door. After putting my neck in a brace, they expertly got an oxygen mask strapped over my face. Still, the problem was my chest. Every breath was agony. Then half lifting and half sliding me they managed to maneuver me onto a stretcher. Looking back I chuckle now when I recall how the emergency crew had to enlist several onlookers to heave me into the ambulance.

My first ride in an ambulance ended at the doors of Saint Francis Hospital. I guess the shock had worn off. My gasping had slowed, but the pain of being moved onto the x-ray table took my breath away once again.

Tests completed, they left me in the emergency room. Soon a mountain of a man, Sargent Dewey of the Highway Patrol, lumbered up to the gurney. Naturally he had a few questions. How fast was I going? What happened? Talking required my full concentration. I fought for breath. He ended mercifully soon with the words, "Damned good thing you had your seat belt on. You'd a gone through the windshield." Even though I knew that he was right, somehow the words proved of slight solace.

When the doctor returned, his verdict hardly surprised me. "Well, nothing much is wrong. You're lucky." Easy for him to say, I thought.

"You've got some hairline fractures on some ribs. Nothing I can do about that. They'll heal on their own, but it will hurt to breathe for sometime." No kidding! "Neck's going to be sore, and you'll have bad bruises from the seat belt. But you should be okay."

My mamma didn't raise me to be impolite, so I mumbled my thanks. Sitting up and putting on my shirt required more concentration. I had to remember to breathe no matter what.

As we drove away, Mark, one of the friends who had come to gather me home, asked, "Do you want to go see your car? We're going to pass right by the garage."

"Yeah, let's see it," my other friend, Rod, replied enthusiastically.

I groaned inside, just wanting to get home, but my curiosity has often been too strong for my own good, so I nodded okay.

My poor little Corolla's front end had been mashed to a third its size. Sargent Dewey hadn't exaggerated. I would have been a goner without my seat belt. Hitting a steel monster at 40 m.p.h. and coming away without worse damage had to be a blessing.

Mark and Rod whistled and shook their heads. "Boy, oh boy. Good thing you had your seat belt on," they concurred.

For the next few weeks breathing started out being agony, but sure enough came back to normal. I guess like most things, I forget how nice it is to breathe. Then I see a bashed car, remember the blue blur, hear the squealing tires, recall the front end of my Corolla, take several, soothing, deep breaths and thank God.

Carl Koch

OUR BREATHING CAN HELP US IN CAP-
TURING OUR MOMENTS. . . . THE
BREATH IS ALWAYS HERE, RIGHT
UNDER OUR NOSES.

Jon Kabat-Zinn

Uncle Joe

As I rode up in the elevator of the VA hospital, sadness washed over me. I knew that the next day when I flew out of Memphis headed for the Philippines that I would probably never see Uncle Joe again. Emphysema had invaded so much of his lungs that now he had to fight for every breath, and Joe didn't have much fight left in him. This had to be his last stand against the disease that had slowly, painfully choked him, now to his death.

I had been delayed getting to the hospital by the last-minute plans before a big trip. Now as I hurried toward his room, the hospital seemed abandoned. Without the periodic garble coming from loud TVs, the floor appeared empty.

The door to Joe's room stood partially open. I poked my head in and met my uncle's startled gaze. His eyes widened when he saw me there, then embarrassment shrouded his face. He was on a portable commode. Too weak to help himself or to get up, he had soiled himself. He tried to speak, but his weakness and the oxygen mask cut off any sound.

"Don't worry, Uncle Joe, I'll get a nurse to help you."

I rushed down the hall to find an aide. I knew that Joe was mortified that I had seen him helplessly smeared in his own excrement. He had always been so in-charge, so forcefully right, so tidy, always the old Air Force master sergeant.

Pretty soon the aide waved me back into Joe's room. I made small talk with him for a few moments. Gasping for breath even with the oxygen mask, he only nodded or answered in monosyllables. Of course neither of us alluded to what had just happened.

My usual ability for gab deserted me. Making nice and offering vacuous pleasantries to someone this close to the gates of heaven just seemed blasphemous. So, daring tears, I finally told Joe what I really had come to say.

"I'm leaving tomorrow for the Philippines. I had to come by to say goodbye. You have been a super uncle to me, Joe."

I watched as his eyes filled with tears. He struggled even harder to breathe.

I hurried on, realizing that I had better get this said before I broke down. "I know that I'll probably never see you again, so I had to tell you that I love you, Joe. I'll miss you like hell. You were always good to us kids and that meant a lot."

By now Joe had grasped my arm, holding firmly to me and nodding even as tears coursed on either side of the mask. He lay back as if collecting himself for a huge effort. I sat there silently praying for his release from this suffering.

"Carl," he gasped, "I loved you and the other kids, too. Damned cigarettes." He stopped to draw in as much air as he could. He clutched my hand now, holding on as if I might leave before he was done.

Pausing often between words, he said, "Promise. Tell Melba, I love her. Always loved her."

"She knows that, Joe. But I promise I'll tell her."

"Promise?"

"As soon as I get home I'll tell her. I'll call her tonight."

He nodded, satisfied. He dropped my hand, exhausted by the effort of his few words. Even though he was fighting for breath, his face seemed calmer.

"Good-bye, Uncle Joe. Thank you. I'll always remember you. Don't worry, I'll tell Aunt Melba." He nodded again, but was clearly drifting off.

At five the next morning, the phone rang. Joe had died a few hours after I left the hospital.

My aunt asked me to sing at Joe's funeral. Rearranging my flights and arrival into Manila was a small price to pay for all the years that Joe and Melba had loved me.

Joel, a good friend from the University, helped me gather a small choir of students. Before the funeral service began, Joel had us warm up and then led us through each of the hymns. Perfectionist that he was he even told us where to breathe. As we worked our way along in "Amazing Grace" I watched this group of young people breathing in unison, wonderfully unconscious of the miracle being performed inside them. My mind flashed back to my uncle gasping and struggling for each precious breath.

The casket arrived at the church door, prayers were offered, and as my family processed in I gratefully took a deep breath and intoned Psalm 23: "My Shepherd is the Lord, there is nothing I shall want." I prayed that Joe was with the Shepherd in those green pastures and that now he had what he so desperately wanted during all those years of decline—eternal breath, everlasting life.

Carl Koch

THE CREATOR FORMED THE FIRST HUMAN BEING OUT OF THE SOIL AND BREATHED THE BREATH OF LIFE INTO THE NOSE OF THIS FIRST HUMAN.

Book of Genesis

Say It Gratefully: I Am a Sexual Being

SEXUALITY IS THAT EMBODIED ENERGY WHICH LINKS US TO OTHERS IN COMMUNICATION AND COMMUNION; IT IS OUR ABILITY TO AFFECT AND BE AFFECTED BY OTHERS.

Kathleen Fischer

Becky was quite simply lovely. Bright brown eyes sparkled. Her skin radiated health. At nearly six feet, she carried herself with a quiet elegance. She was in her Rubenesque phase right now: a bit more rounded than currently the craze. In any case, she hated her body.

We sat at a small table, sipping our coffee. I had come to visit her at the clinic where she was being treated for addiction to diet pills. Far away from home, she eagerly looked forward to our Sunday conversations.

For my part, I found the visits sad, frustrating, and confounding.

Becky would greet me with a warm hug. Since she could not leave the clinic, we would find somewhere on the premises to sit and visit. Over the many weeks that I had been coming, I thought that I saw progress. At each visit, Becky would tell me just a bit more about the traumas of growing up the survivor of repeated rapes by her grandfather.

He had started abusing Becky when she was six and continued until she reached puberty. Her ordeal did not actually end when he died because she hid her secret so deeply that only with the onset of a mental breakdown did it finally let loose.

During therapy for the abuse, her problems with alcohol and diet pills also emerged. She had hit the teen years as a chubby young woman. The weight had been an attempt to repel her grandfather. Of course it had been futile. Then in adolescence the taunts of her peers about her being fat added to her misery. She started taking diet pills to lose weight. When a boy would comment about her nice looks, alarms went off for her. She would gain all the weight back, presuming that her good looks would lead to abuse. For the next thirty years Becky repeated this pattern, eventually adding bouts of binge drinking when stress overwhelmed her.

Her treatment seemed to be helping Becky come forth from the darkness. And so we sat over our coffees, visiting about this and that. Suddenly she looked at me, saying, "God, but I still hate my body. I feel so ugly."

Reaching out, I caressed her forearm lightly. "Becky, come on, you know that you're very pretty."

Her arm stiffened. Though she did not try to remove her arm from my hand, I knew that some terrible memory had scared her.

"Becky, what just happened?"

"That's what he always said right before he abused me."

She started to cry softly, and so did I. Words that were meant to affirm and console held only abuse and hurt for Becky.

Eventually Becky left treatment much more healthy than she came. Though she sometimes has haunting nightmares, most of her life is filled with light now.

This experience with Becky highlighted how important it is that we embrace our sexuality, for if we cannot do that, we cannot love our body either. Not affirming and enjoying our sexuality throws up walls to relationships of all kinds.

Our sexual energy, flowing from our bodyself, is a great gift of creation. Sexual energy urges us to create new friendships, new loves and, for some, offspring. One story that highlights this connection between sexuality and creativity is the biblical account of creation. God said, "I will make human beings in my own image. . . . So God created male and female in the divine image. In the image of God they were created. God blessed them and proclaimed them very good." And in God's image, the two were to imitate God: that is, they were to create new life.

Sexual attraction and pleasure draw us to each other. Without sexual expression we would not survive as a people. That's the plan of creation. Accepting our sexual body then becomes an act of accepting our likeness to the Creator, the Life-Giver; we become life-givers and creators through our wonderful, sexual bodies.

Many of us carry around old messages about the dangers of sexuality. Other messages tell us that sexual expression feels good, so just do it. A more balanced view seems to be that our sexual body is a great treasured gift to be celebrated. Poet Audre Lorde declared that sexuality is "lifeforce" or "that creative energy empowered, the knowledge and use of which we are now reclaiming in our language, our history, our dancing, our loving, our work, our lives."

Now is a good time to empower ourselves. As we grow to love our body, we increasingly embrace our sexuality. And vice versa. This embrace of body and sexuality leads us to wholeness and health. We reclaim our self as a lifeforce.

> SEXUALITY HAS TO DO WITH THE ESSENTIAL PART OF WHO YOU ARE, THAT THING ABOUT US URGING US INTO RELATIONSHIP, INTO COMMUNION, INTO CREATIVITY—WITH OURSELVES, WITH ONE ANOTHER, EVEN WITH GOD.
>
> *Kelly Brown-Douglas*

Say It Gratefully:
I Am a Sexual Being

- Sit in a comfortable chair. Relax. Take some deep breaths. Then ponder these questions:
  - When I was young, what attitudes about sexuality did I learn from important adults in my life?
  - What particular events or conversations do I remember that shaped my attitude towards my sexuality?
  - How do I feel about being naked with other people around?
  - How do I feel now about my sexual body?

- Name your sexual organs and ponder the functions of each one. Even better, stand naked in front of a mirror. Look at yourself, focusing on your sexual organs. How do you feel doing this? Then, consciously, affirm your sexual body in any way you find comfortable or use these affirmations:

  For women:

  - I gladly affirm my body as a woman!
  - I affirm the wonder of my ovaries, my uterus, my clitoris, and my vagina, all wonderful parts of my sexual self!

  For men:

  - I gladly affirm my body as a man!
  - I affirm the wonder of my testes and my penis!

  For women and men:

  - I affirm that my sexuality is life-giving and good!
  - I affirm my desire to nurture and cherish my sexual body!
  - I pledge myself to expressing my sexual self by nourishing strong and loving relationships and by sharing my gifts with other people!

- Spend some time reflecting on these questions: How can I better appreciate my sexuality? Are there particular issues or attitudes about my sexuality that I want to deal with and maybe rethink and revise my perceptions about?

OUR BODILY EXPERIENCE IS ALWAYS SEXUAL. . . . SEXUALITY IS OUR WAY OF BEING IN THE WORLD AS BODY-SELVES.

James Nelson

Black Silk Is Me!

I had eyed the enormous, fancily beribboned box all during my birthday supper: a new winter coat? A quilt? Something we needed for the house, like the planks my husband wrapped up one year, which he later made into a desk for me?

After a round of "Happy Birthday," our two-and-a-half-year-old helped me blow out the candles on my cake and the baby applauded. My husband, George, handed me the package—too light to be wood, not bulky enough for a coat. From clouds of snowy tissue I pulled out a long, black silk nightgown and matching robe.

Oh.

I was taken aback. This was the kind of frippery I brought on my honeymoon, the stuff of newlyweds. What kind of present was a black silk nightgown and robe for the mother of two small children?

I imagined spit-up quickly spoiling the liquid folds. I saw sticky fingers reaching for a lustrous sleeve, spilled juice sopping the hem. Bath water would stain it, toy cars would snag it, baby nail clippers would rip it. It wasn't the sort of robe you pulled on to fetch the morning paper or to go comfort a sick child in the middle of the night. I struggled to mask my disappointment at such useless extravagance. We were on a tight budget, and I really needed a new winter coat.

I left the tags on, intending to return it after tactfully telling George that, although I truly appreciated the gesture, didn't he agree that it was pretty impractical? Somehow, though, I couldn't leave the silky set alone. For one thing, it was gorgeous—not Frederick's-of-Hollywood sexy, but movie star-elegant sexy. The gown's bias cut made it float. The carefully engineered robe had an inner tie around its slightly gathered waist and a generous outer sash to finish into a big, jaunty bow. The coyest bit of black lace edged up each sleeve. Michelle Pfeiffer probably sauntered around her Malibu terrace in an outfit like this, sipping chocolate cappuccino as she gazed dreamily at the Pacific. I liked just knowing I owned such a thing, the way some people revel in the possession of a Belgian-lace tablecloth or a 1921 bottle of Cheval Blanc.

And it felt great. After everyone was in bed that birthday evening, I slipped the garments on, half hoping they'd look better on the hanger than on me so that I'd have a good excuse to give them back. But no. Cut long and loose, of fabric more gossamer than a newborn's hair, the nightgown and robe were unlike anything that had ever brushed against my skin before. Forget garter belts and the Wonderbra. I've never felt so comfortably glamorous in my life.

And because I felt so good, I looked good, too. Or at least that's what my husband thought. "Why don't you dress like this more often?" he asked, only half joking.

I kept the nightgown and robe. And not just for seduction.

Sometimes, after the kids are asleep, I change into the silky set just to read, because it feels so nice. (I stash a flannel robe nearby in case my kids call me in their sleep) After one of those rare evening baths—the luxurious kind I used to take routinely in my childless days, complete with scented moisturizer and time to shave both legs—I'll extend the indulgence afterward by wearing the nightgown and robe even as I fold laundry or pick up stray pieces of cereal.

The bedroom set cheers me even when it's just hanging in my closet between my all-purpose denim dress and my boring navy blazer. A week or a month might go by between wearings, but I know it's there, like an alternate persona I can slip into at will.

In my heart of hearts I know that neither sex nor glamour nor comfort nor the guilty pleasure of conspicuous consumption led me to welcome the black boudoir ensemble to my wardrobe. Rather, it's that just as the nightgown and robe allow me to feel—however fleetingly—like a slinky starlet on the silver screen. The mere fact that my husband picked them out for me means that that's how he sees me, too.

Beneath this harried, flannel-clad, diaper-dispensing exterior still beats the heart of the old sensuous, frivolous me. And being reminded that my husband knows this is the best gift of all.

Paula Spencer

SEXUALITY IS PROFOUNDLY CONNECTED TO NATURE. . . . SEXUAL ENERGY, OR *EROS*, IS LIFE-FORCE THAT PERMEATES ALL OF CREATION AND IS PART OF THE JOYFULNESS OF LIFE CREATION.

Christiane Northrup

Home

I woke refreshed. As I lay in the unfamiliar bed, I luxuriated in the sunshine filling the room. A large vase of orchids stood on the bookcase. Each dusty burgundy blossom was almost as big as my hand. Although the windows shut out the January night, I still felt the sweet, balmy air.

"I'm in Hawaii!" I lay grinning as I pondered having eight days on the Big Island: my brother's guest, alone, without spouse or children or household to look after. An escape, not only from responsibilities, but also from the long, dark Minnesota winter. Jumping out of bed, I was eager to explore.

My brother called, "Come on outside. I want to show you something."

I looked down at the long cotton nightie I was wearing. "Will we run into any people out there?"

"Nah. Just the cows."

When I joined him, he handed me some rubber flip-flops. Then I followed him through the front door, across a muddy driveway, and out to the rutted road. At home I would never walk outside my house without being full dressed, but walking along this road in my nightie seemed surprisingly natural. The rain forest's vegetation released a delicate fragrance. Something primitive nudged to consciousness the feel of my skin wrapped around my frame. My flesh felt vibrantly alive as the soft breeze stroked me.

At the end of the road, my brother pointed out Mauna Kea. "Look. Isn't she beautiful!"

I nodded and smiled. The volcanic mountain peak rose majestic in the distance. But my tingling skin and the exuberant vegetation distracted me powerfully. I heard the familiar-yet-different cooing of a Hawaiian morning dove. The incongruous sight of cows grazing in a pasture bordered by palm trees set me to chuckling.

When we returned to the house, I shed my flip-flops, grabbed a towel, and headed to the shower outside. The stall was in a wooden shed not far from the back door. A big redwood tank nearby caught rain water for the shower. Walking across the wet lawn in my bare feet, I entered the shed, closed the door behind me, slipped off my nightie, and opened the shower curtain. Then I found myself turning around and reopening the shed's door. I didn't want to be separated from the soft morning air. Peeking around to assure myself that I couldn't be seen, I stepped into the shower. Steam filled the room as warm water mingled with the cool outside air. After a luxurious shower, I grudgingly put my nightie back on. I felt wet and tender, like a newborn puppy.

I couldn't bear to go back into the house. My body craved the rich morning sunlight. I roamed my brother's spongy lawn.

Dense vegetation bounded one side of the lot, so I padded over to get a better look. A slight clearing among the palms and ferns invited exploration. Curious, I slipped along the path, keeping alert for unfamiliar tropical creatures. The grass dampened the hem of my nightie. The jungle drew me in. My breath quickened.

I stepped through the curtain of palm leaves into a circular clearing just big enough for me to stand in and turn around. A dome of palm branches filtered out the sky. Sounds were muted. Alone. I was thrilled by this secret spot.

Palm trees with leaves larger than me enclosed the clearing. Ferns of all sizes were tightly curled like the heads of violins, though some unfurled in the soft light. Under my feet, the soil was soft and damp and springy. And I was wet wherever the jungle had touched me.

I began to sway languorously, curving my female body, imitating the unfurled ferns. I danced, turning and turning. A Great Mother lovingly wrapped herself around me.

Yet wildness surged there, too. An aggressive ruthlessness. Raw power to heal or destroy.

I pulled off my nightgown. I stretched my arms above my head and arched my back like a cat waking from a pleasant nap. I felt strong and dangerous and beautiful—a leopard in her lair. I spun faster in my dance, tears streamed down my face. I had come home.

Anne Peek

WHEN YOU OPEN TO THE JOURNEY OF THE BODY YOU OPEN TO A LOVE RELATIONSHIP IN THE BODY THAT OCCURS CELL BY CELL.

Christina Baldwin

URGE AND URGE AND URGE, ALWAYS THE PROCREANT URGE OF THE WORLD,

OUT OF THE DIMNESS OPPOSITE EQUALS ADVANCE, ALWAYS SUBSTANCE AND INCREASE, ALWAYS SEX,

ALWAYS A KNIT OF IDENTITY, ALWAYS DISTINCTION, ALWAYS A BREED OF LIFE.

Walt Whitman

WAY 10:

Learn Something New Every Day

THE MOMENT ONE DEFINITIVE-
LY COMMITS ONESELF, THEN
PROVIDENCE MOVES TOO. . . .
WHATEVER YOU THINK YOU CAN DO
OR BELIEVE YOU CAN DO, BEGIN IT.
ACTION HAS MAGIC, GRACE, AND
POWER IN IT.

Goethe

As part of learning to eat well and to eat right, Joyce and I have been adding more fiber and reducing the amount of fat in our food. Learning to cook differently has been an adventure in itself. I have been trying new pasta and Chinese recipes. Some of my new dishes are more delectable than others. Joyce likes to bake. Of course, baking without sugar and butter presents unique challenges, but also opportunities for creativity.

Our search for low-calorie, high fiber, tasty cookies came up short of our hopes. We found one oatmeal-raisin cookie that met all of our criteria, but two problems hampered our completely embracing these delicacies: availability and price. The store seldom had a supply because they came from a small bakery across the state. And they were expensive.

In our desire to have something sweet to eat, Joyce determined that she could create a cookie just as good. Besides our own desire for having these taste treats, Joyce wanted to bring some healthy goodies to a nursing department meeting. Armed with the ingredients off of the package of our favorite cookies, Joyce gathered the oatmeal, raisins, applesauce, and so on. Using a traditional oatmeal-raisin recipe, she began experimenting.

The first batch seemed a bit too dry, so she added more applesauce. The second batch was moist enough, but the texture felt a bit mushy. She added some flaxseed. The third batch, while different from our store-bought cookies, was marvelous. She's been making these Heil Premium High-Fiber Oatmeal-Raisin Health Cookies ever since, much to my delight and the gratitude of her students and our friends.

Besides providing a healthy and tasty treat, Joyce grew from the experience—and not at the waistline. Let me explain.

While learning and creating, Joyce was—literally—growing into a new person. Research on the brain has shown that new learning physically reorganizes and spurs the development of new connections in our brain. When we are learning and creating, our brain uses the stimulation to reshape itself. Each brain cell takes in, sorts through, and transmits information out of its dendrites to axons that release neurotransmitters through synapses, connecting to other cells. In short, our brain grows. In learning about this new recipe, trying it, making adjustments, trying again, Joyce grew a whole new set of connections in her brain!

All of us have the same opportunity, every day, every minute. To love our body, we need to keep learning. Sure, our body might slow down, but a vital brain makes life vital. Vital people, no matter how short and stout or tall and thin, radiate that vitality to all around them. In this regard I think of my Grandma Werner. She had a hard life raising eight children through the Depression and World War II. As a girl she had been badly burned in a kitchen fire. Well into her sixties she broke her back in an auto accident and suffered through a southern summer in a body cast. I don't remember seeing Granny read anything besides the newspaper, but her mind stayed busy by keeping track of the large family, tending her roses, and especially by playing cards. Every week she played bridge with the same group of "girls." In between bridge sessions, she played canasta and other card games with anyone she could corral. Granny would gather my cousins, my sister, and me around the kitchen table. Sipping a beer, munching on sliced cheddar cheese and raw onions on saltines, she presided at the end of the table, her bright eyes watching our every move. Granny always won, but then she always kept score. Granny died at age ninety-five, a year or so after the last of the "girls" had passed on. She had no one with whom to play bridge anymore. Some of us kids opined that she would be in heaven bragging to the "girls" that she had outlasted them all.

Researchers have concluded that deteriorating health, particularly in older people, can often be correlated to the stagnation of their minds. "Use it or lose it" applies here. Some research has even suggested that helping people exercise their learning may slow the progression of Alzheimer's. Our mind can keep growing and expanding all through life if we stay interested in life. Nurturing our mind can be done in a wide variety of ways: reading, writing our memoirs or journaling, quilting, taking piano or computer lessons, planting a rock garden, taking up power walking. My father took a biochemistry class when he was sixty-five. Colleges now welcome people of all ages.

We can feed our brain every day. Feeding our brain nourishes our whole body. The Buddha declared, "All that we are is the result of what we have thought. The mind is everything. What we think, we become." We now have scientific evidence of what the Buddha knew those many centuries past.

One of the most important ways of learning is creating. The creative act really gets our brain cells going. In the Judeo-Christian tradition, God's first act was creating the universe. Specifically, God created women and men in the divine likeness. So, we were created to be creators. We are meant to bring new things into being, whether that means developing a new oatmeal-raisin cookie, designing a more comfortable chair, breeding a new pansy, or rearranging our closet for greater efficiency. Each act of creation means that we learn new things in the process of making something new.

Someone once asked the then elderly American poet Henry Wadsworth Longfellow how it was that he had maintained his vigor for so long. Pointing to a nearby apple tree, he replied, "That tree is very old, but I never saw prettier blossoms on it than it now bears. That tree grows new wood each year. Like that apple tree, I try to grow a little new wood each year." We are never too old to learn and create. Here are a few examples:

At age seventy, Noah Webster published his two volume *An American Dictionary of the English Language.*

Having suffered a stroke at age fifty-two, Handel still completed *Messiah*, which debuted when he was fifty-seven.

Mary Baker Eddy started *The Christian Science Monitor* at age eighty-seven.

At age eighty-four, Agatha Cristie monitored the making of the movie *Murder on the Orient Express* based on her novel.

Toni Morrison won the Pulitzer Prize for *Beloved* when she was fifty-seven and received the Nobel Prize for Literature at sixty-two.

Betty Ford opened her clinic for substance abusers at age sixty-four.

At forty, John Glenn took his first orbit of the earth in space. He made his most recent orbit on the space shuttle at age seventy-seven.

So, take a huge step in loving your body by learning something new every day. Take a new route to work. Read an editorial that you ordinarily skip. Find a new website about fiber in food. Start writing a journal. Plant some new seeds. Your brain will grow. You will become healthier and more vital.

QUESTION: DO YOU KNOW HOW OLD I'LL BE BY THE TIME I LEARN TO PLAY THE PIANO? ANSWER: THE SAME AGE YOU WILL BE IF YOU DON'T.

Julia Cameron

Learn Something New Every Day

- Without censoring yourself, quickly write twenty "wishes"—things that you wish you could do. Don't leave anything off the list just because some nagging voice says it is silly. Start each wish with the words, "I wish." Leave your list for a day or so. Then take it out. Pick one item and begin learning to do it. Remember that you learn little by little. So if you want to learn to play the piano, find a piano teacher. This may mean calling friends and asking if they know a teacher. In other words, intentionally take the small steps towards your goal.

- Make another list of fifteen little changes that you would like to make in your life: for example, turn an old stool into a plant stand by painting it bright red, eat thirty grams of fiber every day, read some inspirational passage each day, and so on. Each week select one of the changes and begin doing it over that week. Each change will invite new learning and creativity—new brainpower!

- At the end of each day, consciously record at least one new thing that you learned that day no matter how seemingly insignificant. Keep a journal of learnings, or at least tell your spouse or God what you learned. This will reinforce your practice of learning something new every day.

LEARNING IS EVER IN THE FRESH-
NESS OF ITS YOUTH, EVEN FOR THE
OLD.

Aeschylus

Dear Jane

Both Joyce and I are teachers. We admire diligent students. However, the learning we are describing here has more to do with keeping our minds open and hearts ready to expand by seeing fresh possibilities where others see only difficulties. Learning then becomes a creative adventure that literally causes our brains to grow. Paradoxically, when people approach learning as a fearful endeavor and sheer drudgery, the brain actually reacts by shutting down connections.

*A person with an open mind can learn anywhere, any-
time. All of life becomes an opportunity to see more clearly.
Duke Ellington once remarked, "I merely took the energy it
takes to pout and wrote some blues." Our perceptions expand
when we take the energy that "it takes to pout" and use it to
grow. Thankfully, Jane, the subject of the following story,
eventually learned this lesson.*

Jane pulled up in front of my office building at the
university right at noon. Typical. Only a tornado or
an unavoidable pileup would stop her from being on
time for any appointment. What was different about
her though was that she jumped out of a sleek, cherry
red convertible with its top down. Granted it was pre-
owned, but the Jane of two years ago drove a conserva-
tive brown VW Fox.

As Jane walked towards me I relished the sight of
her now. She strode towards me. Her smile stretched
impishly from ear to ear. Even though she wore a loose
flowery blouse over her rumpled jeans, I could tell that
she had lost some weight. Bare toes stuck out of aged
sandals. Relaxed. Confident. A far different Jane
walked into my hug.

A few years before, when Jane paraded across the
stage at her college graduation, the president applauded her right after announcing that Jane was ranked first
in her class, having maintained a perfect 4.0 average as
an electrical engineering major. She added that Jane
had accepted a doctoral fellowship at Georgia Institute
of Technology.

Jane's parents, Bob and Sue, stood with me as we
cheered and applauded that day. Tears streamed down
their smiling faces. I choked up to see these two dear
friends of mine—Bob and I taught at this same university—so proud and gratified. While Bob never pushed
Jane, he steadfastly encouraged and guided her when
she asked for help. Sue never went to college, but she
appreciated what Jane had accomplished.

Even while we cheered, I knew that some measure of worry lurked just below the surface of our joy. Jane had been a large intellectual fish in a small departmental pond. The engineering department was good, but not first rate. Jane had brains to burn, but she would meet grad students at Georgia Tech who were smarter than she was and who had come from more competitive schools. We wondered if Jane could stand up to grades less than an A. After all, from pre-school through university, Jane had never received any grade lower than an A. An added worry was that Jane spent so much time studying that she never exercised and had only one or two friends. She had the pale looks and pudgy frame of an inveterate bookworm. And so, we wondered.

The frantic phone calls started soon after the first semester began at Georgia Tech. "Dad, I got a C on my first test. God, I can't believe it. I studied for days and was sure I had it down pat." Bob and Sue consoled her, reminding her of the competition and that she couldn't expect A's. A few days later, Jane cried over the phone, "These guys are so brilliant. Why did it take me so long to see that I'm so stupid? They seem to breeze through all the work. I'm getting two and three hours of sleep just to keep up."

At midterm, Bob and Sue drove the eight hours to Atlanta to visit Jane. They returned home more worried than I had ever seen them.

"Carl, she's gained tons of weight. She's eating junk, never goes out, and has bags under her eyes. I know she can't be sleeping much. Her room is a pigsty, if you can believe that. Weekends, she holes up in her room or at a lab somewhere and works. She's going to crack. I just know it." Sue's stunned look mirrored her words.

Bob was no better off. "She talks about coming back home and going back to the university here. I know they would take her back in a minute with a full ride.

They had her teaching some labs even last year. But, I hate to see her leave feeling like a failure. If she could only be realistic! She raved that she was going to fail every course when she's actually getting a couple of A's and B's in the other two courses. Where did she get it in her head that she couldn't get B's? Maybe I pushed her too much."

The agony for all of us continued until Christmas. When Jane drove up her parents' driveway, she brought with her the entire contents of her apartment. She said she could not go back, would not go back. For two days she barely came out of her room. Bob and Sue could hear her crying. They held back. Waiting. Hoping that a little time and distance would help her come back to life.

Jane's siblings, Sarah, Pete, and Sam, and their families came into town for the holidays. They were good medicine for Jane. With a combination of teasing, listening, and sibling advice, they drew her out. Sam, the only one in the family not to be a valedictorian, maybe helped the most. What he lacked in counseling technique was more than made up for by his love of his sister and his understanding of her unrelenting perfectionism. His cajoling increased when Jane's grade report finally arrived in the mail: two A's and two B's.

"Get over it, toots. So you got a couple of B's. You think that anybody gives a damn? Hell, all those aerospace companies you want to play engineer for could care less. They'll line up to hire a woman."

Jane loosened up, but decided to return to the familiar turf of her alma mater's engineering department. She also started counseling with a wise friend of Sue's. Time and good help healed. Jane starred again in the department. Her undergraduate lab students loved her. She even began to date.

When Jane polished off her thesis and passed her exams, offers poured in from Ph.D. programs and corporations. To everyone's surprise, except Sam's, she took a job with an aerospace company that sent her five hundred miles away. But this time when she went away, Bob and Sue smiled. Gradually, in small ways, they saw that Jane could now occasionally accept less than perfection.

Jane and I were finishing our iced tea, which we needed to ease back the bite of the fajitas. My curiosity had gotten the better of me. "Jane, what in the world is in that bag you dragged in here? A present for your adopted uncle maybe?"

"I was wondering how long it would take you to ask. You're getting more patient in your old age." She did know me.

Picking up the bag, she lifted out something smothered in bubble-wrap and began to unwind it. It was a ceramic pot. When she sat it down, it wobbled on its base. "I made this just for you. I'm still learning, as you can see. So don't put anything in it or it will dump over."

I lifted the pot up. Truly it was a beginner's effort. The enamel had run where it should not have. The top was uneven. But to me it was beautiful. My face gave away my joy and pride.

"You know, Uncle Carl, I could never have even thought of giving you something flawed like this two years ago. I would have trashed it and waited until I could make something perfect. Well, I'm learning that it's okay to be less than a Walking A Average. Crazy too, I'm having more fun and actually doing better work without all that weight I laid on myself. There's so much I want to learn now, and I can because I know learning is a journey, not a report card." She paused. Her eyes had started to fill with tears. We smiled and nodded. Then grinning, she waved at the waiter, "I think we need some lime sherbet to top this celebration off."

Carl Koch

WHY SHOULD WE ALL USE OUR
CREATIVE POWER. . . ? BECAUSE
THERE IS NOTHING THAT MAKES
PEOPLE SO GENEROUS, JOYFUL,
LIVELY, BOLD AND COMPASSIONATE,
SO INDIFFERENT TO FIGHTING AND
THE ACCUMULATION OF OBJECTS
AND MONEY.

Brenda Ueland

Dancing to a Different Reflection

When I first read this story of discovery, I thought of another story about creativity. Donatello, the great Italian sculptor, had a huge block of marble delivered to him. After carefully examining it, he told the workers to take it away because it had too many flaws. The men groaned at the idea of rolling the enormous piece of marble all the way back to the quarry. So they cleverly decided to see if the sculptor down the street, Michelangelo, would take it. He was so forgetful that he wouldn't remember that he had never even ordered it. Sure enough the sculptor looked it over and had them leave it. Michelangelo saw all the defects that Donatello had seen. He also saw his David standing in the block of marble. Creators and learners like Michelangelo and Kellie Mincer Rosenfeld, described below, see opportunities for beauty and growth where others see only defects and difficulties.

"**D**ance Dimension's" recital was well into its second hour when Ginny's mind began to wander. She had lost count of the ballerinas, gymnasts, and tap dancers who had graced the stage since her four-year-old daughter, Lindsay, had performed. So she decided to amuse herself by reading the names on the program. Ginny was almost finished with the roster for the tenth act when her mother leaned over and whispered in her ear.

"Look at that chubby ballerina," she said in her most disapproving tone. Her mother's caustic remark made Ginny quickly look up from her program. She focused once again on the stage, where ten nine-year-olds were lined up, each one dressed in pale pink. It didn't take long for Ginny to figure out which ballerina her mother was talking about.

The "chubby" ballerina didn't look much different from the other nine-year-olds on the stage. She was dressed in the same pink leotard, with a ring of tulle encircling her waist. Her blonde hair was gathered into a bun, and a pink ribbon, similar to the other girls' ribbons, was tied around it. The only difference between her and the other ballerinas was her size. Her legs were heavy under her white tights, and the leotard she wore highlighted her round body.

This unusual ballerina was indeed "chubby." Ginny cringed as she thought of that word. She could remember the humiliation of looking through the Sears catalog with her mother, trying to find an outfit they both liked in the "chubby" section. "Look," her mother would exclaim, "the vertical stripes on this jumper would make you look so much slimmer." Ginny would agree with her mother and order the vertical stripes, even though she really wanted the dress with the red polka dots that she had seen in the "regular" girls' section. Even now that she was grown up and had a daughter of her own, she still wore only vertical stripes. Horizontal stripes had never touched Ginny's ample body.

"She's a brave little girl," Ginny whispered to her mother, as they watched this special ballerina prance across the stage. She was a natural performer. She smiled as she showcased her talent, reveling in the attention. She twirled and stepped gracefully in time to the music, obviously not worried about how she looked in the tutu. Ginny admired the self-confidence that this girl obviously possessed.

I wish I could have been like that when I was young, Ginny thought to herself. As a preteen, Ginny had hidden in her room, listening to music, reading fashion magazines, and dreaming of the day when she would be thin like the models she saw pictured. When a favorite song would come on the radio, Ginny would get up and twirl around in front of her full-length mirror, pretending that she was a famous dancer. But Ginny hadn't dared to take dance lessons. She was too afraid of what the other girls would say if they saw her in the form-fitting outfit dancers were required to wear. Ginny now realized that if she hadn't been so afraid of what others would think of her large size, she could have had more fun. She could have learned to dance.

Ginny didn't dare to share this personal regret with her size eight mother. Like many large women, Ginny avoided discussing fat acceptance with anyone who bragged that she had gained only five pounds since her wedding forty years ago. And, besides, she knew any discussion they had about weight would be about losing it, not accepting it.

As an adult, Ginny thought she had learned to like her natural weight, but now she realized that she still hid her shape from the outside world as much as possible. Ginny recalled with shame the hours she had spent in department stores looking for the least revealing tent-like garment to hide her ample figure. Heaven forbid that her dress should fit like a glove!

How she envied the young ballerina's bravery, nine years old and twirling on the stage for all the world to see. And Ginny still wore black because it was slimming, although red was her favorite color. As Ginny watched her gracefully glide across the stage, she wondered if the girl was too young to realize that people could be cruel to the weight-challenged, or if she was just too happy dancing to care. Ginny watched her laugh with joy as she twirled, showing a hunger for life. This special ballerina was a beautiful dancer.

The music stopped and the audience began to applaud. Tears came to Ginny's eyes as the little girl smiled and took her bow along with the others. As Ginny watched her skip off the stage in triumph, she realized what she had to do. She leaned over to her mother and said, "Tomorrow I'm going to buy a leotard."

"What in the world for?" her mother gasped. "Someone of your size would look dreadful in a leotard. Where would you wear it?"

"To dance class, Mom," Ginny answered. "I'll never be nine again, and I'll never be thin, but I can be a dancer."

Kellie Mincer Rosenfeld

IT IS THE CREATIVE POTENTIAL
ITSELF IN HUMAN BEINGS THAT IS
THE IMAGE OF GOD.

Mary Daly

WAY 11:

Choose to Be Hopeful, Help Others, Be Grateful

EVERY SMALL, POSITIVE CHANGE WE
CAN MAKE IN OURSELVES REPAYS US
IN CONFIDENCE IN THE FUTURE.

Alice Walker

For over a year now, I have been a "buddy" to a grandmother living with the AIDS virus. I've begun to wonder who is helping whom. Lily (I have changed her name and other details to protect her privacy) seems to have contracted the virus through a transfusion. Incredibly, she has been living with the disease for nearly fifteen years. Lily only found out that she had the virus two years ago when she developed the pneumonia that is often the harbinger of the conditions associated with HIV/AIDS.

Lily's life has been anything but easy. She grew up with her grandmother, a cook for a wealthy family, because her mother and father could not take care of her. As a teen, she returned to the parents she hardly knew. Life with them was filled with arguments, fighting, and booze, but somehow Lily made it through high school. This ended her education. She went to work immediately.

Her three children proved to be the only blessing from a marriage that went sour. Her husband abused Lily and the children. In a courageous move, Lily left her husband. She moved with the children to a small city six hours away from him and began a new life. She worked hard. The kids worked, too. Money was tight, but somehow Lily managed to get her kids through high school.

Lily loves her children, but she has few illusions about them. Two daughters have had children out of wedlock with men who ended up being a lot like Lily's former husband, abusive. A son has two children that he is raising more or less on his own. Then, Lily found out that she had HIV.

When she left the hospital after over a month recovering from pneumonia, Lily had to stop work. Her doctor put her on a rigid regime of drugs to control the HIV and the attendant infections. Officially disabled, Lily lives on the small check she gets at the start of each month and relies on food stamps, which she hoards so that she can buy necessities toward the end of the month. Living in subsidized housing helps a lot.

So what does this story about Lily have to do with loving our body? Simply said, our attitude toward life in general has an unmistakable, scientifically proven effect on the health of our body. I'm convinced that Lily's hopeful spirit, kindness to others, and consistent attitude of gratitude probably kept the illness away for so long. As I get to know her better I suspect that the joy she takes in her five grandchildren, in budding redwoods, and in a good cup of coffee will help her live longer than anyone expects.

Lily is a woman who delights in the many little gifts that I mostly take for granted. When I take her out for lunch, we always go to the same café. She loves the coffee there and takes indescribable delight in the french fries. When she showed me pictures of her newborn granddaughter, her oohing and aahing made me laugh and brought smiling, knowing glances from an elderly woman at the next table. When she moved into public housing so that she could live with her daughter and two of her grandkids, she never complained about it being inconveniently on the edge of the city. Instead Lily boasted about how close the apartment was to the bus line and how great it was that she had a chance to walk.

When I take Lily shopping, I am amazed at her joy when she finds bargain prices for macaroni and cheese. Several days each week, feeling ill or well, Lily looks after one of her granddaughters, loving this time they have together. When Lily goes to support group meetings, she listens and laughs, encourages and advises those living with HIV/AIDS; she's a grandmother to them all. She even helps train volunteers like me.

Lily is good for my heart. Whenever I drop her off and carry her groceries into the apartment, I leave feeling lighter. Despite her poverty, illness, worries over her kids, the rigid regime of her medications, Lily smiles readily, takes delight wherever it can be found, is always grateful, and does what she can to help.

Heart health and body acceptance are as much about hopefulness, delighting in life's gifts, offering kindness, and having a grateful attitude as they are about avoiding fat and cholesterol, doing aerobics, and staying rail thin. After all, Lily stands maybe four feet ten. She has a round face and round figure. Because of age and HIV, she walks with a bit of a shuffle. But people who know Lily don't see someone too short or too pudgy. They see life and goodness.

Blind and deaf, Helen Keller once advised, "I have walked with people whose eyes are full of light but who see nothing in woods, sea or sky, nothing in the city street, nothing in books. What a witless masquerade is this seeing. It were better far to sail forever in the night of blindness with sense and feeling and mind than to be thus content with the mere act of seeing."

In her book, *Growing in Hope*, Lou Anne Tighe describes hope as "the peculiar human ability . . . the transcendent capacity in every human being that, assisted by God's grace, can look beyond the limits of the present and envision a future . . . life in abundance." What people like Lily and Helen Keller realize is that life right now is abundant if we choose to see with hope and delight and gratitude. Even if we are short, poor, and HIV positive; even if we are blind and deaf.

Oliver Wendell Holmes once said,

> If anyone should give me a dish of sand and tell me there were particles of iron in it, I might look for them with my eyes, and search for them with my clumsy fingers, and be unable to detect them; but let me take a magnet and sweep through it, and how it would draw to itself the almost invisible particles by mere power of attraction. The unthankful heart, like my finger in the sand, discovers no mercies; but let the thankful heart sweep through the day, and as the magnet finds the iron, so it will find in every hour some heavenly blessing. Only the iron in God's hand is as precious as gold.

Our body is a precious treasure. As we decide to see with a hopeful heart and give thanks for all the gifts of life, we can more and more take joy in this body of ours.

MY JOYS HERE ARE GREAT, BECAUSE
THEY ARE VERY SIMPLE AND SPRING
FROM THE EVERLASTING ELEMENTS:

THE PURE AIR, THE SUN, THE SEA
AND THE WHEATEN LOAF.

Nikos Kazantzakis

Choose to Be Hopeful, Help Others, Be Grateful

- We can choose to be hopeful about loving our body and about life in general. Our hopefulness grows by every small decision that we make. As Alice Walker advises, "Every small, positive change we can make in ourselves repays us in confidence in the future." Today, every day, is a chance to act hopefully, to make one small, positive change. Try reading some hopeful passages or quotations for a few minutes in the morning. Pray a morning prayer or sing a line from a hopeful song as you drive to work. Consciously ask for help to let go of an old grudge. Decide to praise someone that you would usually like to criticize. Remember that when we plant an act, we reap a habit. What small, positive change can you make today to plant a habit of hopefulness in your life?

- Compassion for other people can teach us compassion and love of ourselves, too. One of the great paradoxes of life is that accepting and even embracing the limitations and weakness of others helps us accept and embrace our own limitations and weaknesses. And vice versa! Who is calling for your compassion? Consider people close at hand in your family, among your neighbors, or the people you work with.

- Start keeping a "Day Blessings" journal. Every night before you go to bed, write down at least one blessing from the day.

> ALL OTHER PLEASURES AND POSSES-
> SIONS PALE INTO NOTHINGNESS
> BEFORE SERVICE WHICH IS REN-
> DERED IN A SPIRIT OF JOY.
>
> *Mohandas K. Gandhi*

Fernie and Fran

Our friend Fran religiously had her pap smears and mammograms. She walked every day, ate well, and stayed healthy. But always in the back of her mind was a frightening fact: her mother and two sisters had died of breast cancer. Now she sat in the oncologist's office, weeping, scared, angry, and confused. Even though she had come to the doctor as soon as she discovered suspicious lumps, the doctor wanted to do surgery.

Julie, Fran's doctor, had suggested that she get a second opinion about surgery. The second doctor, Dr. Morris, agreed. "Fran, I'm sorry, but given your family history, I recommend surgery and a regime of chemotherapy. You caught it in good time, so I'm optimistic, but this is a safer way to go."

Bill, Fran's husband, heard the news and was determined to be brave for her. Choking back his own tears, he said, "We'll get through this, Frannie. I'll be with you the whole time." And he was.

The doctors tried to reassure Fran and Bill that the surgery had gone well, that the cancer seemed to have been contained, and that Fran's recovery should go as hoped for. Nevertheless, when she lost her hair during chemo and had to stay in bed, weak and nauseous, Fran grew depressed. Even after the chemo ended and her hair had grown to crewcut length, Fran stayed list-less. As Bill dressed to go to work every day, Fran hud-dled under the blankets. Bill wondered if he had made a mistake in encouraging Fran to retire at sixty from her accounting job. Maybe if she were still working, he thought, she would have a reason to get up.

The doctor, Bill, and some of Fran's women friends encouraged her to join a support group of breast cancer survivors. Fran put them off, "I'm not ready yet." Bill's concern grew as the weeks passed.

One morning as Bill drank his coffee, sitting alone at the breakfast table as usual now, he noticed an article in the newspaper about therapy dogs. Instead of breezing through the article, he read it word for word. A therapy dog, he learned, was a dog especially trained to visit the sick and elderly for the sole purpose of cheering them up. All that day and the next couple of days, Bill kept thinking about the article. A plan was forming in Bill's mind.

Then one night, as supper grew cold, Fran heard the garage door open. Bill was late for about the third time this week. Fran was building up steam to scold Bill when the door flew open and a blur of furry creature danced across the slick kitchen floor and slid into her. In a whirl of golden fur, tale waging frantically, a dog nuzzled Fran's hand and then stood up to lick her face.

"What! What!" was all Fran could get out.

Bill struggled into the kitchen with bags of dog food, a bowl, and sacks of treats. "Meet Dorothy."

"Dorothy! My God, that's a terrible name."

"Well, you think of a good name because she's yours."

"I could kill you, Bill. We don't need a dog around here. Besides I'm not up to it."

"I couldn't leave her at the pound, could I? Now that the kids are gone, we need somebody to take care of."

And so Dorothy eventually became Fernie, though the source of the name was a mystery even to Fran and Bill. Not as mysterious was the gradual effect Fernie had on Fran. Now she had to get up to let Fernie out, to feed her, and to make sure she had her walk. Soon Fran had regained some spring in her step, color in her face, and laughter in her voice.

Also as part of his plan, Bill kept bringing up therapy dogs and how golden retrievers were ideal to cheer up others who were down. One night Fran had had enough. "You're not so damned subtle," she said. "So how does Fernie become a therapy dog anyway?"

Months later after some training, Fernie nosed her way into Sarah's room at the nursing home. Fran followed the golden retriever in but was surprised to see that the bed was empty. All of Sarah's personal items had vanished: the stuffed dog that Sarah always held, the pictures of her great-grandkids, and the wilting balloons from her ninety-third birthday party. All gone.

As if she knew what had occurred, Fernie whimpered and then pawed the bed. Fran wept. After she cried for a while, Fran led Fernie down to the nurses' station.

Fran was consoled by the charge nurse, Alice, who told her that Sarah had died about a week before, just after Fran and Fernie's last visit. Alice hugged Fran. After a few moments, she stood back and looked at Fran and Fernie. "What a team you two are! You know, I think Sarah waited till your visit before she let go. Each time Fernie and you visited Sarah seemed to come back to life. You know what else, when she died, she had that stuffed dog in her arms. We all swore that she was smiling."

Fran smiled weakly and then looked down at Fernie. "Well, girly, we still have rounds to make. Let's go see Ms. Davis." As if she understood exactly, Fernie leapt to her feet and started tugging Fran down the hall.

Carl Koch

"IF THERE IS RIGHTEOUSNESS IN THE
HEART, THERE WILL BE BEAUTY IN
THE CHARACTER. IF THERE IS BEAU-
TY IN THE CHARACTER, THERE WILL
BE HARMONY IN THE HOME. IF
THERE IS HARMONY IN THE HOME,
THERE WILL BE ORDER IN THE
NATION. IF THERE WILL BE ORDER IN
THE NATION, THERE WILL BE PEACE
IN THE WORLD."

Anonymous, Chinese

Mrs. Higgins

In 1966, between my sophomore and junior year in college, I took a bus to Chicago with a group of other university students to organize a rent strike against one of the worst slumlords in the city, much to the horror of my folks. Even though I had taken part in civil rights actions before with all the fervor of a new convert to religion, this trip took me into more dangerous territory in their minds. After all, I had been born and raised in Memphis where, a couple of years later, Dr. King would be gunned down. At college I had experienced a conversion through my growing friendship with Jim Smith and Dick Mann, two African-Americans who destroyed all the stereotypes from which my prejudices sprang.

My zeal had an angry edge to it. Every door I knocked on, every strike pledge I got seemed a personal salvo against racism. Now that I look back on it, I realize that these were strikes against my own sense of guilt, too. My intolerance of intolerance knew few bounds. Then I encountered Mrs. Higgins.

I had been prowling through the decaying build-ings, getting signatures to support the rent strike. Strangely, we all wore ties to give the petition drive an aura of respectability I suppose. At the time I weighed in at about 250 pounds—about fifty pounds too much. I was wilting in the heat, foot sore, and sweaty. Mrs. Higgins' apartment was up three flights of stairs that reeked of urine and stale cooking odors. In the late afternoon meltdown, I just wanted to go to the dorm we were staying in and have a long shower and a cold drink.

So when I knocked on the last door for the day I almost hoped that nobody would answer. Then I heard a slow shuffling of feet, the fumbled unlatching of four different locks, and the opening door hitting the chain. The wrinkled face of a small, old woman peered out of the apartment.

"Hello," she smiled. "Can I help you?"

I gave my pitch about the rent strike. Her kind eyes never left my face.

When I finished my speech, she said, "You look real hot. Would you like some lemonade? It'll make you feel lots better. Come in, won't you, and sit down."

Surprised and relieved, I assented. I was desperate-ly thirsty, and Mrs. Higgins had an indefinable quality about her that made me feel comfortable and at home. Most of the paint inside her apartment had faded. The ancient furniture was threadbare, but the whole place had a well-scrubbed cleanliness about it.

Mrs. Higgins asked me where I was from. I halting-ly replied, "Memphis."

"I come from a sharecropper's farm down near Tunica, Mississippi, not far from Memphis."

We talked about southern places and things for a while and then about the civil rights movement, which Mrs. Higgins took keen interest in.

Then she said, "You know, I understand why so many of these black kids are so angry." Her voice grew somber, and her eyes looked beyond me into a long distant past. I felt my body tense.

"I used to hate white people," she said softly. "For years I did. You see, when I was a little girl we'd all go out to chop cotton—my mama, sisters, and brothers. This one day, the sun was just about killing everybody, but we had to keep working. The landowner drove up in his truck. He was a bad man. He came over to my mama and started yelling and grabbing at her arm. I couldn't hear what they said. I was too far away. My mama was a proud woman and didn't take shoving from nobody. I yelled and started running to her. Next thing I know, that white man had snatched up the hoe she'd been using and was hitting her with it. Again and again. Some of the other people tried to stop him, but it was too late."

Her mother lingered for a day before she died. The killer never got charged with the murder. Mrs. Higgins paused and breathed deeply, as if the effort of the telling had worn her out. I sat stiffly on the edge of the couch, sad, embarrassed, and ready to flee.

"I held onto my hate for whites like a greedy man holds to gold. It ate on me and ate on me. Then about twenty years ago, I finally heard the words of Jesus about forgiveness and love. I'd been so sour on the world. I'd been miserable in my own self. Then and there I pledged to Jesus that I better stop hating white people.

"Let me get you some more lemonade."

As she took my glass to be refilled in the kitchen, I sat stunned. This old, poor woman had found forgiveness for herself and for her ancient enemy. I cannot completely explain it, but I felt forgiven too. If she could forgive the man who killed her mama, maybe I could forgive myself and learn to love as she did. Tension drained out of me. My shoulders loosened.

I left the apartment, strike petition forgotten. Mrs. Higgins had lifted a burden off of my shoulders, lightened my load. The heat and tiredness seemed to vanish. The day suddenly felt like spring. Mrs. Higgins had given me something of infinitely more value than her signature: hope.

Carl Koch

HOPES ARE WHITE STONES SHINING UP FROM THE BOTTOM OF POOLS, AND EVERY CLEAR DAY WE REACH IN UP TO THE SHOULDER, SELECTING A FEW AND REARRANGING OTHERS, DRAWING OUR ARMS SMOOTHLY BACK INTO AIR, LEAVING NO SCAR ON THE WATER.

Natalie Kusz

You're Never Too Young to Grow Old Gracefully

IT'S NOT HOW OLD YOU ARE, BUT

HOW YOU ARE OLD THAT COUNTS.

Anonymous Octogenarian

The moment we emerge from the womb, we begin aging. We are taking our first motions leading to death.

Now I know that this sort of statement might come off as a downer, even if we know that it's true. However, the sooner we can embrace this idea, the sooner we can start living in the real world and making vital decisions, namely: How am I going to live my life so that when I am old I will not look back with regrets? In short, how am I going to live till I die?

Most of us have known thirty-year-olds going on ninety, and ninety-year-olds going on thirty. We know people physically young who have all the worn-out looks, forgetful minds, and stooped bodies that we stereotypically associate with our elders, and some of us are fortunate to know elders who maintain energetic schedules, sharp wits, and vigorous strides.

In *Hospitals and Health Networks* newsletter, Chris Serb recounts preparing a ninety-four-year-old Alaskan Athabascan Indian for a cardiac stress test. Serb inquired of the seemingly fit gentleman about any problems that he might be having. Looking at Serb, the elder answered seriously that recently he had been getting tired after only fifteen miles of checking out his trap lines, walking on snowshoes and packing all of his gear.

Most research about aging indicates that most gracefully aging people don't suddenly wake up at age sixty-five and say, "I'm going to start changing my life. I'm going to have a wonderful time growing older!" Instead, most people who age with grace have been making positive, life-giving choices throughout the course of their lives. The Athabascan elder did not start his strenuous life when he retired. More likely than not he had been vigorous, active, engaged for all of his ninety-four years.

We all have the same choice that Maurice Goudeket talks about in his book *The Delights of Growing Old*: "I get up before anyone else in my household, not because sleep has deserted me in my advancing years, but because an intense eagerness to live draws me from my bed." Such intense eagerness is nourished and developed by each decision for life that we make when we're twenty, thirty, forty, fifty, and sixty. Even if we haven't always made the best decisions to nurture our health, we can now.

Take for example hairdresser AnnMarie De Monte of Bloomfield, Connecticut. She lost her father to a massive cardiac when she was in her mid-thirties. Having become sedentary herself and never having any encouragement to exercise regularly, AnnMarie nevertheless started jogging with a group of friends. At first, she wondered if she wouldn't have a heart attack herself, but in the course of time, she began racing. Then she started competing in triathlons.

By her mid-forties, AnnMarie felt ready to take on the Hawaiian Ironman Triathlon World Championship. Contestants had to swim over two miles, bike 112 miles, and run a 26.2-mile marathon. At her tenth Ironman, she took first place among women fifty-five to fifty-nine.

In her mid-thirties, AnnMarie De Monte chose to live. We all need to select our own ways of living till we die. On a radio talk show, the host asked a 102-year-old man how he faced life every day. In a steady voice, he replied, "Every morning when I get out of bed, I have two choices: to be happy or to be unhappy. I always choose to be happy." And why not?

Well into his eighties, actor Hume Cronyn kept up a regular schedule of moviemaking. He certainly did not need the money or more awards. Acting gave him energy and purpose, and he gave all of us a gift through his performances. He told an interviewer, "I just can't sit and contemplate my navel hour after hour. I think actually if one could arrange one's parting as happily and easily as possible, it would be while holding the hand of someone you loved and in the middle of some real involvement with life."

Actress Bette Davis is quoted as saying, "Old age is not for sissies." Indeed, it is not, because to grow old with grace and liveliness means that we make positive choices to engage with life. To dance with the possibilities of the day. To bring the body we have to life through walking, eating well, playing with our family, and challenging our brains. To make the choices to grow old gracefully at whatever age we are.

A REPORTER ONCE ASKED THE
WORLD-RENOWNED CELLIST PABLO

Casals, "You are ninety-five now and acclaimed as the greatest cellist that ever lived. Why do you still practice six hours a day?"

Stopping, putting down his bow, Casals answered, "Because I think I'm making progress."

You're Never Too Young to Grow Old Gracefully

- When Supreme Court Justice Hugo Black was seventy-five years old, a reporter asked him if the rumors of his retirement were true. Black looked at his watch and told the reporter that he didn't have time to talk because he was on his way to play a set of doubles. Black had his way of staying vigorous and alive. What is your way?

- Some statements that are commonly used to describe good health habits are listed below. Ask yourself how you are doing in each area. If you are doing okay, be thankful. If you want to make some modifications, jot down some action steps that you can take: be sure that they are realistic.

  - I eat healthy foods, especially vegetables, fruit, whole-grain, high fiber breads and cereals, lean meat, and low-fat dairy products.

  - I limit my consumption of fats and cholesterol-rich foods.

- I exercise for twenty to thirty minutes at least three times each week.
- I maintain a healthy weight.
- I enjoy sufficient quality time with family and friends.
- I don't smoke and stay away from smoky environments.
- I'm a moderate drinker of alcoholic beverages, if I drink at all.
- I have developed leisure activities that I find relaxing and energizing.
- I keep track of medications that I take and do what I can to need less and less of them.
- I try to bring joy and meaning to my work.
- I express my feelings clearly, but appropriately, rather than swallowing them.
- I have learned stress-reducing strategies.
- I wear a seat belt and drive safely.
- I read and try to keep learning.
- I pray and reflect regularly.

- The *Serenity Prayer* is best known as the prayer of people in twelve-step recovery programs, but it contains a wisdom helpful to all of us. It says:

  "God, grant me
  the serenity to accept the things I cannot change,
  the courage to change the things I can,
  and the wisdom to know the difference."

  In choosing to embrace life until you die, to enjoy and nurture your bodyself, reflect again on:

  - the things about your body that you cannot change

- the things that you can change
- the areas where you need wisdom to know the difference.

Consider making the *Serenity Prayer* a daily practice. As you say the prayer, ask

- for serenity about those aspects of your body-self that you will need to live with until you die,
- courage to change what you can change so that life will be healthier and more full, and the wisdom to know the difference.

- Imagine what you would like to see your body look like in five years. Either draw a picture or write a description of "my bodyself in five years." Ponder the decisions you are making to have this body.

- List five affirming statements that remind you of the goodness of your body: for example, "I am the Creator's work of art," or "I am enough, and I have enough." Every morning read at least one of these affirmations.

I WISH I KNEW WHAT PEOPLE MEAN WHEN THEY SAY THEY FIND 'EMPTINESS' IN THIS WONDERFUL ADVENTURE OF LIVING, WHICH SEEMS TO ME TO PILE UP ITS GLORIES LIKE AN HORIZON-WIDE SUNSET AS THE LIGHT DECLINES. I'M AFRAID I'M AN INCORRIGIBLE LIFE-LOVER AND LIFE-WONDERER AND ADVENTURER.

Edith Wharton

If I Can Do It, Anyone Can

Certainly for me, the key to a fulfilling old age is staying independent. Though I'm eighty-two on the surface, I feel about fifty inside. I feel mature enough to know how difficult life has been, but young enough to start doing new things.

By nature I am very independent, and still do my own housework except cleaning the windows, as my children have persuaded me that climbing isn't such a good idea. My doctor doesn't understand this attitude, and offers all sorts of help, which I don't need. My response is to say that when I do need it, I will ask, and then I will expect it to be available.

Old age is a time of great opportunity. A positive mental attitude is more important than being strong physically, and perhaps it's something you're born with or learn at a young age. I know people who say that they would love to do something new, but they can't. If someone says I shouldn't be doing something I ask why not. If I want to do something I will and nobody will stop me. Now people don't argue with me any more.

I went back to college when I was seventy-six and ended up with two degrees and an A level in English. During my time there I also learned that young people are far nicer than they are usually portrayed, and I had more kindness from them than from many people of my own age. I'm known a little bit for what I've been doing, but people associate studying at my age with not learning properly as a child. We all have to carry on learning throughout our lives, and you can't just stop at thirteen or fourteen as many people did.

At college nearly all the other students were eighteen or nineteen. When I went into that class for the first time we all had doubts about each other, but by the end of the first lesson I was accepted as one of them. They could see that I could stand up for myself and that I wasn't asking for any favors because of my age. Recently three of the girls came up to see me because they remembered it was my birthday; they visited for five hours.

I would like to see groups set up to help older people find out what they can do. Some would need a lot of help, but it would be so worthwhile in the end. You can feel a little bit lazy when you don't want to do something, but you have to make the effort. If you stop trying you're on the slippery slope.

I've always been a strong person. When I was a child and my mother was ill I would stay up all night and look after her; when the cat had to be taken to the vet I would do it. My mother inherited her emotional strength from her family, and my governess had it too. She would take me to libraries and museums and said that one day I would be famous. But it was hard to believe that when I was searching under stalls for cast off vegetables. Life has not been easy, and I did every job I could before I was married and when my children were growing up.

Though the medical profession has improved its attitude towards older people, there are still too many practitioners who treat you as a child. But people of seventy or eighty are not kids any more. You can read the impatience in people's faces just because you might need to use a cane for walking. Do we give this picture to the world? Is this what they see? After all this effort, do I look like an idiot just because I've got a cane?

I wrote three short stories in 1990, which were broadcast on the radio, and now I'm writing a book. It's a semi-autobiography that includes my childhood years. I've written seven chapters so far. But I do realize that my time is limited—I can't say that I've got ten years, or five years or even two—so I have to get on with it now. When I was young my headmistress told me that she thought I would write a book, and I'm still going to be here for the launch.

There's nothing older people can't do if they put their minds to it. Most people will already have done the really hard things like bringing up children, looking after them when they're ill, and helping them learn to read. After that, doing a few lessons is easy. There's nothing special about me; if I can do it, anyone can.

Katherine Harris

IF ONE IS NOT TO PLEASE ONESELF
IN OLD AGE, WHEN IS ONE TO
PLEASE ONESELF?

Vita Sackville-West

Better With Age

My friend is turning forty, certainly a momentous occasion to be celebrated. We no longer suffer from teenage hormones. The angst of "What do I do with myself?" has subsided. We are accomplished and healthy and strong. And I want to find her a birthday card that celebrates all this and more.

Instead, all I see are cards that make getting older sound like a disease: jokes about flatulence, droopy breasts, incontinence, memory loss, and lousy sex lives. At the other end of the spectrum are sappy odes more fitting for white-haired grandmas in rocking chairs and sensible shoes. (Who buys these cards, I don't know, since I know of no grandmothers these days who fit that description.)

Today, we live longer due to exercise, better nutrition, and medical advances, yet sadly, as these ridiculous cards reveal, our perceptions of growing older have not caught up with these realities. Isn't it time we started to acknowledge the joy of becoming a mature adult in modern society?

At twenty, I was insecure about my abilities and future, extremely lonely, and did incredibly stupid things that still make me blanch with shame. I wasted a lot of precious time whining over things that I now know do not matter. But as I matured, I gained a husband and son I adore, a solid circle of friends who have stayed the course, and a satisfying career. I've developed enough self-restraint not to make an idiot of myself (well, not usually) and the ability to more easily ride out the hard knocks of life and savor its pleasures. My experiences have a deeper, more meaningful hue. I anticipate that the knowledge I have yet to gain will make the rest of my life equally rich.

Getting older no longer means empty days, scanning the obituary pages in the newspaper, and waiting for the kids to call. My sixty-nine-year-old mother works out three times a week, recently published a book, and teaches at a world-renowned botanical garden. She may wear sensible shoes, but that's because canoeing down the Amazon River wearing heels is just plain nuts. In his seventies, my father still practiced medicine, could talk the stuffing out of anyone in a political discussion, and did the crossword puzzle in the magazine section of *The New York Times* every Sunday (in ink, yet).

Both my mother-in-law and father-in-law can fix cars and re-shingle roofs, and leave the rest of us behind when we go cross-country skiing.

None of them are unique. Just look around: today it's not uncommon for women to have children in their forties and even fifties. John Glenn went back into space at the age of seventy-seven. The Rolling Stones, in their fifties, still command audiences of hundreds of thousands after thirty years of touring.

So why isn't any of this vitality reflected in the culture around us? Ironically, while we are able to live active lives longer, society keeps lowering the bar that defines "old." Products are marketed solely to the eighteen to thirty-four-year-old crowd, as if life loses all value once you hit thirty-five. Corporate executives, who were once esteemed for their expertise and loyalty, are now unceremoniously given their walking papers in their forties, traded in for younger, less expensive colleagues. Fourteen-year-old supermodels hold up barely pubescent figures as ideals that many older women distressingly feel the need to emulate.

Unfortunately, in our visual society, perception tends to become reality: If we are told someone is incapable or without worth just because of age, we treat them that way and they become that way. It's a self-fulfilling prophecy—and a tragic waste of knowledge and potential. Our problems as a society are too vast, too complex, to sideline such a large, experienced, and willing population just because of preconceived notions.

Isn't it time that our negative beliefs caught up with the joyous reality of getting older in this day and age? We need to explode this demoralizing, destructive myth perpetuated about the aging process and finally start celebrating the rewards of maturity. Instead of rejecting those with laugh lines and gray hairs, let's embrace them for what they truly are: symbols of great national resources—wisdom, knowledge, strength, and ability.

Beth Levine

WE ARE THE CREATOR'S WORK OF ART, CREATED FOR THE GOOD WORKS WHICH GOD HAS ALREADY DESIGNATED TO MAKE UP OUR WAY OF LIFE.

Letter to the Ephesians

ACKNOWLEDGMENTS

"The Wisdom to Know the Difference" on pages 14-17 and "Abundance" on pages 75-78. Rosalie Hooper-Thomas is a writer and consultant to businesses. She and her husband live in West Salem, WI.

"Not Everyone Can Be Big-Busted—Shall We Get On With Our Lives?" on page 28-31. Leslie Knowlton's story originally appeared in *Cosmopolitan*. Used with permission.

"Birthing a New Self-Image" on pages 31-33, the story of the man with one leg on page 50-51, "Dancing My Way Home" on pages 87-90, and "Home" on pages 114-117. Author Anne Peek is an attorney, a busy mother, and likes to dance. Used with permission.

"A Rose by Any Other Name" on pages 42-44. Rose Kreutz, the subject of the story, is a professor of nursing at Viterbo University in La Crosse, WI. Used with permission.

"Consider the Lilies" on pages 45-47 by Barbara Brown Taylor. Copyright © 1999 Christian Century Foundation. Reprinted with permission from the October 6, 1999, issue of the *Christian Century*.

"Our Perfect Bodies" on pages 54-56. Anne Symonds' article first appeared in *American Health*. It is used here with her permission.

"I'm No Susan Sarandon" on pages 57-59 by Barbara Matson is reprinted with permission of *Family Circle Magazine*.

"Stop and Smell the Crayons (Walking With a Five-Year-Old)" on pages 64-67 originally appeared in *Woman's Day*; "Black Silk Is Me!" on pages 112-114 first appeared in *Parents Magazine*. Both articles are used with Paula Spencer's permission.

"The Healing Touch of a Generous Woman" on pages 67-69 by Marilyn Greenberg is reprinted with permission of *Family Circle Magazine*.

"Early Morning Offerings" on pages 90-93 by Phyllis Theroux originally appeared in *House Beautiful* and is used with permission.

"Dancing to a Different Reflection" on pages 129-132 by Kellie Mincer Rosenfeld first appeared in *Radiance* magazine.

"If I Can Do It, Anyone Can" on pages 151-153. Katherine Harris's story is used with permission of the British Medical Journal Corporation.

"Better with Age" on pages 153-155 is used with permission. Beth Levine is a freelance writer whose work has appeared in many national magazines. She is the author of *Divorce: Young People Caught in the Middle* and co-author of *Playgroups: A Complete Guide for Parents*.

CARL KOCH currently serves as an adjunct professor at the Graduate School of Saint Mary's University in Minnesota, teaching in the Master of Arts Human Development program and the Doctor of Education Leadership program. He has authored and edited many books on prayer and spirituality, including high school textbooks.

JOYCE HEIL, who received a master's degree in nursing from Saint Louis University, is an assistant professor of nursing at Viterbo University.

KOCH AND HEIL are married and live in Onalaska, Wisconsin, where they enjoy swimming, walking, cooking, and eating!